PLAYING CHARADES
WITH THE DECEASED

Michelle Meleo

Cheyenne

Enjoy Playing Charades!

♥ Michelle Meleo

Copyright © 2014 Michelle C. Meleo

ISBN:1495941590
ISBN-13:978-1495941597

DEDICATION

Dedicated in loving memory to my sister Margo.
You are forever in my heart and welcome to play
charades with me anytime!

Margo Meleo
October 1, 1974 – June 4, 1992

*I'm sure that our souls have met before and that we
will find each other again in the afterlife.*

CONTENTS

Acknowledgments   i

1   Child's Play   Pg 1

2   Developing Your Skills   Pg 11

3   Messages vs. Imagination   Pg 23

4   What They Want us to Know   Pg 33

5   All Are Welcome to Play   Pg 49

6   Negative Spirit Energy   Pg 59

7   Protection and Preparation   Pg 71

8   Tools of the Trade   Pg 91

9   Are You Ready to Play?   Pg 115

10 Advanced Development   Pg 133

    About the Author   Pg 147

    Afterword   Pg 149

ACKNOWLEDGMENTS

I would like to first and foremost thank my husband David. It is not an easy task to live with someone who walks with one foot in the spirit world and one in life. I am forever grateful for your unconditional support and love.

To my parents.
You guided me in the right direction without any former training. You taught me to trust – while learning it for yourselves and you loved me unconditionally no matter what. All of these traits have been an invaluable part of who I am and has helped me develop my psychic abilities. "Thank You" from the bottom of my heart, you are my heroes.

To Diane,
For your loving input and editing of the book, for raising your son to be the man of my dreams and especially for being you.

To you the reader,
I believe that there are no mistakes in life and even if our paths have crossed by way of this book, you were destined to read it for one reason or another. I thank you for your support, your courage and for the loved ones that have led you here.

Chapter 1
CHILD'S PLAY

My earliest memories of the deceased making an attempt to communicate with me was when I was around eight years old. I remember lying awake in my bed, filled with the fear that the nightly visitors would hurt me in some way.

They would always come out when it was dark and at the time when I was halfway between the worlds of dreamland and being awake. I would see movements out of the corner of my eye, hear the shuffling of feet and loud whispers of people shouting single words into my left ear. Words like "HEY!" and "MICHELLE!".

At this tender age, I had no idea that I was

communicating with the spirit world and would cover myself with a blanket all the way up over my head, leaving only a tiny opening for me to poke my nose and eyes out of. I would even cover my ears to block the occasional yelling into my left ear.

They came to visit me every night and they all seemed to want to tell me something important...to communicate with me in some way, but I didn't know why. I only knew for sure that they were dead – that they would come to me at night – and that they scared the living crap out of me to the point that I would not sleep without a light on.

They never tried to hurt me in any way and I never actually felt them touching me. I think that somehow they knew that I was frightened but could not resist their need to make contact with me.

I suppose that the constant exposure to these nightly, unexplainable visits had numbed my fears to an extent. I got used to seeing the shadows from the corner of my eye, the whispers in my left ear and the overall sense that I was not alone in my room at night.

As I grew older my fear began turn to curiosity. By age twelve that curiosity had become insatiable and I'd spend most of my free time trying to figure out what they wanted from me.

I did all of this so called "research" during the daytime of course, since I was still secretly terrified of the dark. I experimented with seances, using the Ouija Board and candle divination.

I would employ the assistance of my younger brother, Derek, and sister, Margo. Pulling them quickly into my new obsession with the afterlife.

We mostly used the Ouija board to make our contact with the spirits and it didn't take long for all three of us to be hooked on a daily routine of attempting to make contact with the spirit world.

We would sit around in a circle, following the directions provided on the inside of the game box. We asked questions of the spirits that would make contact with us, most of which were children with ages close to our own. In the beginning, the contact we made was innocent and lighthearted. We had lots of fun learning all about our new spirit friends.

One day, however, things turned around and what was once fun and innocent, turned into something that you'd see in a horror movie (or so we thought). The once good messages of getting to know you turned to messages of threats from spirits with the most unusual names – non-human names.

We were at the point that all three of us were afraid to be alone in the house and sleep evaded us. It was time to get rid of the Ouija Board for good!

The flying shot glass

One of my most memorable Ouija board experiences was what I like to call "The Shot Glass Experiment". The shot glass experiment wasn't really a planned experiment, in fact it was born out of desperation. After numerous contacts with the ghosts that we believed were haunting our house, Derek, Margo and I were beginning to experience a type of mass hysteria amongst ourselves.

The more we used the board, the more negative

the messages would become and before we knew it strange, poltergeist type things were occurring.

Things would move on their own. We would hear banging sounds throughout the house (and always in rooms that we were not in).

We were freaked out on a regular basis. In an attempt to calm us from our fears and anxieties, and in order to re-gain control of her hysterical children, our mother threw away the Ouija board for good. I can't say as I blame her. I mean we were out of control! Informing her that we had inside knowledge that our home was haunted and that Satan himself held the deed to it! Not to mention our constant screaming and running from invisible intruders.

I'd have done the same thing if I were my mother. As I look back now and laugh about it all, I can see why she was so frustrated with us and that damn Ouija board!

"Now what are we to do?" I asked my brother in disbelief that my only connection to the other side had been tossed in the trash. He had the perfect solution to my problem though, and suggested that we make a homemade board out of cardboard and use a shot-glass as the pointer.

And so we went straight to work on creating the shot-glass experiment.

When it was finished we went to it, much like little addicts looking to get our fix of the paranormal. There was no blessing of the board or calling in our guides to protect us before beginning. We were on a mission and we didn't know any better.

The three of us sat at the table around the board. Each of us placed a couple of fingers on the rim of the shot-glass that had been turned upside down on the homemade board and we began. I asked if there was anyone in the room with us and the shot-glass went flying out from under our fingers across the board, then clear across the table finally landing somewhere in the middle of the kitchen floor.

It wasn't thrown. It slid around as if there were invisible fingers guiding it. My sister ran out of the room screaming and crying. She never touched a Ouija board again. As for my brother and me, well we just thought it was the coolest thing in the world. Nevertheless, we didn't use the Ouija board much after that. We were a little freaked out.

It wasn't long after that I'd decided to focus my attentions more on learning to read the Tarot cards. They would be "safe" for me to use and I figured that I'd be better off to step back from the ghost hunting for a while. I had acquired a Tarot deck that had been previously gifted to my mother by my psychic aunt, who was convinced that my mother had "the gift" and insisted she learn to read them.

The Tarot deck, sat unopened in a cupboard until the day I asked her to give them to me so I could learn how to do readings.

She agreed (probably in hopes that it would occupy me enough not to build another homemade Ouija Board, and not so long after, I began reading for family and friends. During readings for my high school friends, spirits of deceased loved ones would come through and make themselves known.

I didn't really like that much and whenever a spirit came through I would keep the message short and sweet by acknowledging that they were there and moving on with the traditional safe Tarot reading.

By the end of high school, I had lost interest completely in knowing what the ghosts wanted and instead just wanted them to go away. I had developed an interesting method to block them out. I had started smoking marijuana and for about a year, smoked lots and lots of it.

I had inadvertently discovered that if I got really stoned before bedtime, it would dull my connection enough so that I could get a peaceful night's sleep. I also found it quite enjoyable during daytime hours and since my friends at the time were all doing it as well, I thought to myself...why not?

Marijuana was a savior for me at that time in my life. It was a short lived savior and fortunately for me, never led to more serious drugs. My parents will tell you that those were my rebellious days.

So if you are one of those people who believe that drugs can enhance and amplify your psychic connection, I'm here to tell you firsthand that drugs and alcohol will surely block any psychic connection that you are attempting to make. I also would like to stress the importance to not make the mistake of thinking that you can use drugs or alcohol as a tool to disconnect your energy from the spirit world. There are safer and more effective ways to do this that I'll outline for you later in this book.

That said...

If ever there was a time in my life that I wanted to turn my back on my gift, it would have been during this time in my life. I had been unsuccessful at finding out what the spirits wanted with me, my friends thought I was a bit freaky, I couldn't understand why they showed themselves and spoke only to me and besides, they still scared the living crap out of me.

I was raised Roman Catholic with a strong belief that this type of communication was a form of communicating with the devil and as much as I tried, I was not able to fully turn it off. This "gift" prompted me to question my religious beliefs for many years thereafter, all the while I stuffed my spiritual connection deep into the back-burner of my life.

It wasn't until my early twenties that I was able to fully understand this gift and how to effectively make a connection with the deceased.

I spent years reading books on the subject. I researched the phenomenon, conducted more of my own research and began to surround myself with people who had similar interests as me.

In the '90's I had begun to apply what I learned by offering my services through a local new age store where I worked.

My dearest friend Sha and I worked at this

place together. Sha and I had gone to grade school and high school together. Although we were friendly with one another in school it was ten years after graduation before we realized how much we had in common.

We started teaching classes at this new age store. It became important to me to share what I had learned with others so they could know and understand how to properly use their own skills. After all, I didn't want others to make the same mistakes that I had made so many years ago.

It had been a long time since I used marijuana to disconnect from the spirit world. I made sure to clear and protect my own energy on a regular basis and prior to making contact with spirits. I began to ask the spirits what they wanted from me and they in turn would tell me.

It took me a long time to learn how to translate the images, feelings and thought sounds that were sent to me from beyond, but once I educated myself and learned how to properly use my gifts, I was able to let go of the fear and open my heart to it.

I found that the more I allowed the deceased to communicate with me instead of blocking them out that the messages would become clearer and I would get better at it.

I also found that by protecting my personal energy I was able to control and only attract spirits of a higher vibrational level. The nightly visits from spirits would lessen and I was able to finally sleep.

I'd constantly find myself in situations where the deceased would come forward to connect with their loved ones giving messages of hope and comfort.

If you are interested in communicating with the deceased, this book will help you find your way. I suggest that you learn everything you can about your gifts so that you are educated and protected before you begin and that you use what resonates with you and leave what does not.

It is my hope that by sharing my journey, you can somehow find your way too!

PLAYING CHARADES WITH THE DECEASED

Chapter 2
DEVELOPING YOUR SKILLS

When was the last time you played charades with someone?

For me, communicating with the deceased can be best compared to a good game of charades. In real charades, the rules are simple: One player acts out a word or phrase by miming/using gestures for the other player or players. You can get as creative as you'd like but you are not able to speak.

Meanwhile, the other player or players try and guess what the first player is acting out.

Playing charades with the deceased is similar with the exception of the way that the clues are delivered. Since a deceased person is obviously without a body, communication must be created on an inner level. In order to communicate, we must be able to experience the clues by seeing with our imaginative eye, hearing with our hearts and feeling from the depths of our soul.

Think for a moment about how you would choose to communicate with someone if you no longer had a physical body to make words, yet you were able to show them gestures in their mind's eye, allow them to experience physical sensations in their own body from you or feel emotions that you send to them.

When a spirit communicates with me they are acting out a scene in my mind's eye. They are the first player and I am the one who is guessing what they are trying to convey. It is really quite amazing to be involved in such an important game.

At first contact, the deceased will usually show me an abstract image.

That image reflects in my mind's eye much like a memory does. In other words, I see it as if I am remembering it. I am able to recognize it as a message from the spirit world because I know it is not my memory. My mind sees the image (or images) as the deceased remembered it from their life.

When reading for others, a deceased loved one will almost always show me an object to prove to their loved one that it is really them.

Usually the object will hold a special meaning for the person that the deceased loved one is trying to make a connection with and can be something as simple as a single object like a coin or a piece of jewelry, or can be as complicated as an event held dear to them.

A repetitive image to search for Mom

During a home party a couple of years ago, I had a young man come through who wanted to connect with his mother. There were many people in line for readings that night and in an attempt to make sure that everyone would be able to get one I quickly set up and called in the first person to be read.

Almost immediately, I saw a broken tree branch hanging over the hood of a car in my mind and asked the person sitting across from me if this had any meaning for her. She said that it did not and we continued on with her reading. When the next person came in for their reading I saw the tree branch once again. Only this time it was a bit stronger and clearer . More details of a tragic car accident began to unfold like a story in my mind. I knew that this was a spirit attempting to come through and connect with someone who was at this home party.

I described what I was seeing once again and asked if it had any meaning for her. She also said that it did not and I proceeded with her reading.

By the time the third person had come in for their reading, the image was coming through so strong that it was blocking any other psychic images from coming in. Much like the other before her, I was not able to confirm that the image I was seeing made sense to her and was stumped as to why this was happening!

Then I sensed a young man standing behind my right shoulder. He then flashed an image of his face into my mind and let me know that he had passed in the car wreck that I had been seeing over and over throughout the night.

He began jumping up and down and pointing towards the living room where everyone had gathered to chit chat, and wait for their turn to see me. I had an overwhelming feeling that I needed to connect him with his mother.

I was not able to finish the reading for the woman who had been sitting across from me (it had already been a few minutes that we sat in silence). So I asked her if she wouldn't mind waiting until the next turn and that I would go and find his mother to give her a reading first. She agreed and we both proceeded to the living room.

Upon entering the living room I immediately found my way to the hostess, doing my best to explain to her what was going. Trying not to sound absolutely crazy, I told her that there was a young man trying to make contact with his mother. I then explained that he would not allow me to concentrate enough to do a reading for anyone but her.

I asked her if anyone who was waiting for a reading had lost a son to a car accident. We went through the long list of people on the reading list *and none of them had. I was really stumped at this point and was beginning to worry that I would not be able to do anymore readings for the night.*

As a last resort, we made an announcement to the group asking if anyone had lost a son to a car accident. I'll never forget the look on his mother's face when she realized that I was looking for her. She was not scheduled for a reading with me that night and was just saying her goodbyes and getting ready to leave for the night. We had found her just in time.

I asked her to sit privately with me for just a few minutes as her son showed me an image of a set of holiday knick knacks arranged on a fireplace mantle. This was his attempt to let his mother know that it was really him.

As it turned out, his mother had not recovered emotionally from the loss and was planning on canceling her usual holiday gathering at their home. The young man wanted to let her know that he was okay and that it was important to him that his family gather for the holiday and that he would be there in spirit.

What an honor it was to bring closure to both of them and help them connect in such an unusual way. I often think to myself what would have happened if I simply ignored those images from the young man that night. (I didn't charge her for the reading by the way.)

Some of the other ways that spirits will communicate with me is through feelings and words. Feeling makes sense right? We know how to feel and can understand how it would work. When we meet someone for the first time we get a "feeling" one way or another. We know straight off if we like them (feel good about them) or do not (an uneasy feeling.)

Sometimes I can feel what a person was feeling emotionally or physically at the time of their death. Usually the feeling is simple and painless and I'll get a general feeling in a specific area. On occasion, the feelings can be quite intense and I'll feel it just as the deceased did when they were living!

A murder victim comes forward

While doing a house clearing for a friend, I had one of these intense occasions. If you are not familiar with a house clearing, it is the practice of removing negative energies from a home, filling the home with positive energy and sealing it in white light.

This friend was a fellow psychic and since her home had just been cleared, we decided it would be a safe place to make some spirit contact together. I had brought an item with me from a client who was hoping to get a message from her niece who had gone missing many years before.

The other psychic and I sat together in silent meditation for a few minutes asking this woman to come forward. Almost immediately, I got a sharp pain in my side. It was so intense that it brought me to my knees. I knew that I had been stabbed with a knife of some sort. Since there was no physical knife present, I knew it was this woman coming forward.

Then I felt another stab, and another. I cannot honestly say how many stabs there were – only that there were multiple. My body hurt and my thoughts were fuzzy.

I began to look around in my mind's eye, making note of her surroundings by describing them to my friend who was really quite freaked out by the whole experience and was encouraging me to close the connection.

This is what I saw through the memories of this woman:

- *I(she) was outside, in the woods somewhere, lying on the ground and it is nighttime.*

- *When I(she) looked up, I(she) could see the back of a blue pick-up truck with the words FORD along the back.*

- *Someone lifted me(her) off the ground and put me in the truck bed.*

- *He was male and I(she) could see the underside of a beard.*

- *I feel like I(she) knew him.*

- *I also get the feeling that I(she) had passed by now because the pain had gone away.*

- *For some reason, my(her) spirit didn't leave*

my body.

- *He drove me(her) somewhere – I'm not sure how long we drove, but I know we are moving fast, as if on a highway.*

After that, the visions go black and I get a sense of where she was left. I get the feeling that it is a landfill of some sort and it is surely gated. I know there are bright lights around it. The woman begins to pull her energy back and I come back to myself.

As I recall this experience, I can see everything again as if it were yesterday – even though the story that I'm sharing with you happened more than ten years ago. I suppose that once you share energy with another, the connection is always there.

Her body has still not been found, but I was able to relay the information back to her loved one and confirmed some suspicions about what happened to her. I still send light to her spirit, in hopes that they will find her someday.

On rare occasions, the deceased will attempt to make physical contact with us. Some examples of physical contact can include feeling pressure on the body, objects that mysteriously move on their own and the ability to see the deceased as if they were standing right in front of you in human form.

Personal assistance from Grandpa

It was a cold winter's day in New England when my youngest daughter Alicia and myself witnessed a physical contact from a deceased relative. Alicia was around nine years old at the time. Being the youngest and with her older brother and sister at the ages where they would spend more time out with friends, Alicia would frequently find herself bored and looking for me to entertain her.

On this particular day, she wanted to play outside in the snow and I was quite honestly not in the mood. I had envisioned a day where the two of us would snuggle on the couch drinking hot cocoa while watching movies together. In an attempt to allow her to get her desire to play in the snow satisfied (while allowing me to stay in the warmth of the house) I suggested that she take a walk outside to check the mail.

Our mailbox was not far from the house at all, but I figured that it would suffice as an outing for her since most of her outdoor ventures for that time of year would only last 10 minutes at most and end on the couch, enjoying the hot cocoa. She was happy with the compromise and eagerly bundled up to head out on her 30 foot long winter journey to the mailbox.

I watched her from the large picture window in the dining room as I had so many times before. On her return trip back to the house however, her foot caught a patch of ice and I watched in helpless horror as both her legs slipped out from under her.

She was falling backwards and I thought for sure she'd hit the back of her head on the brick walkway beneath her. If you have ever slipped on an ice patch before you know how quickly things can happen and I knew there would be no way I could make it outside in time to catch her. I prepared to dart out the door anyway but in the seconds it took for all of this to occur, I noticed that she hadn't fallen all the way to the ground. Instead, her body seemed to gently glide back to an upright standing position.

I stood there...frozen in time looking out that window and watched in amazement as she turned around almost as if she was looking at someone and then dart for the front door.

She ran into my arms and was crying by this time. She said that a man had caught her from behind as she fell backwards cupping his hands under her arms to support her. He then helped her back to her feet. When she turned around to thank him, he asked her if she was alright and she said yes.

Alicia then started for the front door and when she looked back only seconds later, the man was gone. I asked her to describe him to me since I did not see a man in the driveway and I certainly didn't see anyone there to catch her fall. She described her paternal grandfather in exact detail to pictures that I had seen of him from years ago. I showed her pictures of him to confirm that he was the one that helped her in the driveway.

Most might think that a child of her age would

make up a story based on photos or memories of a grandparent and had I not seen it with my own eyes I might agree. But this was different. Different because my husband's father had died long before we were married and I myself had never met him. In fact, my mother-in-law at the time had remarried when her children were young and her then husband had raised the children as his own.

We decided not to tell the children about their blood related paternal grandfather until they were older so as not to confuse them. Alicia had no idea that the man she was pointing out to me in the photo was in fact her grandfather.

The deceased will make contact with us in any way that you will allow yourself to receive the information. If you would like to be open to receive these messages, you only need to be still, open your heart and listen.

PLAYING CHARADES WITH THE DECEASED

Chapter 3
MESSAGES VS. IMAGINATION

One of the most common questions that I get from the living is "How do I know if the messages I get are real or in my imagination?"

It took me more than twenty years to fully develop and understand what was going on with me and for many of those years I wondered the same thing. I wondered if I was just imagining it all in my head. There were even some rare occasions when I wondered if I was not mentally stable. At that time in my life, I didn't know of anyone else who had spirits communicate with them on a regular basis.

But I found that the more I developed this skill, the better I was at determining what was real and what was imagined. In fact, *most* of the time I found these messages to be quite real and would get confirmations from both the deceased that I had communicated with and the living that were longing for answers.

Over the course of time I had developed a method that worked for me. A method that made it easy for me to make a good solid connection and receive confirmation almost immediately that the information I was receiving was real and now I always trust it, even if it does not make sense to the person I am reading for at the time. Because, eventually it does and they always come back to give me confirmation.

The development of these methods were established by trial and error and from actual communications with the deceased. It was during my psychic readings that I would learn how to decipher the messages from the deceased and deliver them to their living relatives.

Only recently have I "publicly" announced that I can and will communicate with the deceased professionally, even though I have done it for most of my life. Prior to this public announcement, I'd just allow the messages from the deceased to come through during my readings, if they wanted to and counted it as an extra bonus for the person getting the reading.

Most of the time deceased loved ones will still come through during a reading. There are also many occasions when they come through at the most inopportune times. Either way, I now always know when it is a spirit and when it is not.

So, how do I know if the messages coming through are coming from a soul or from my own imagination? For me, there are a few signs that I look for and I have been aware of them for so long now that it comes naturally for me.

The first and easiest way for me to determine whether a message was coming from my imagination, or from the deceased, was to learn to read my own memories. When the deceased communicate with me, they do so by sending me images and feelings of their own memories. It only made sense to learn what my own inner experience felt, looked and sounded like, so I would have a comparison.

Next, I learned what it was like for me to read another person's memory of an event. This helped me to get in touch with what it looks, feels and sounds like on the inside of someone else's story.

Finally, I learned what it was like for me to imagine an untrue story so that I could get in touch with the inner feeling associated with that.

By doing this, I was able to build a three point comparison for me to use as a guide during my readings that would help me determine whether the inner experience was my own, another person's or imagined. I'll explain this method to you in more detail later on. Hopefully it can help you to build your own confidence in trusting the information.

Another method I use to help me determine whether a message is real or my imagination is to ask for confirmations or signs. Confirmations can come in many ways and can be as unique as your individuality allows.

The first confirmation that I will always get is in the very beginning of a reading. The deceased will usually show me an object that has significant meaning to the person that I am reading for. These objects are almost always so unique that even the biggest skeptic cannot deny that it is their deceased loved one making contact with them.

Undeniable confirmation from granny

I had a young woman sit with me not too long ago for a reading. She had never had one before and was a little skeptical about the whole idea. Her boyfriend's mother had insisted that she get one and she had reluctantly agreed. It is not one of my favorite things to do – give a reading for someone who is reluctant, but after talking with her for a few minutes, I realized that she was at least curious and agreed to give her the reading.

The reading itself was pretty basic. Talks of college, young love, etc. Towards the end of her reading, however, her grandmother came through to send her a message. She didn't stay long or say much but held out her hand to her granddaughter. She was showing me a set of car keys.

The keys were hung on a very distinct keyring, which I described to the young woman. Then her grandmother told her "here, they are yours now".

As it turns out, her grandmother had willed her car to her, when she died.

I think it's safe for me to say that this woman is no longer a skeptic and was thrilled that her grandmother came through to say hello.

Spirit Bumps

Have you ever had an occasion where chills would run up the back of your neck and you just knew it was a spirit brushing up against you? Feeling this type of confirmation is the most common way to recognize spirit energy. My guides tell me that this happens when they touch you with their energy or brush up against you. They do this to let you know that they are there.

When I am communicating with the deceased for someone and the person is either talking about or asking a question to their deceased loved one, oftentimes I will get chills up my arms to signify that their loved one is agreeing with them. These chills can be so intense that the hair on my arms will stand up and you can see physical goosebumps.

I believe that it is the spirit brushing their energy up my arms to confirm that they are present. I like to call this response my spirit bumps. If you'd like to learn what your physical response will be when you communicate with the deceased simply ask them to touch your energy as a confirmation that they are there with you. I assure you that you will feel *something* and as you communicate more, the feeling will grow stronger.

Some other physical responses that people get

can include; hot flashes, feeling a cold spot or coolness around your body, a feeling of euphoria and some people are even able to feel physical touches from the deceased. This is only a small list of the most common responses that you can feel in your body and as I stated before, you will soon learn your confirmations and your own personal experience with them can be as unique as you are.

Verbal Confirmation

If you've ever watched a professional medium you may have noticed that they will ask the living to verify that they are in contact with their loved one by asking things like "Did your grandmother ever cook with you?" or "Was your father in the military?"

Once a confirmation is made from the living with a simple yes answer, the connection to the deceased becomes stronger to allow for more detailed information to come through. It can be best compared to opening a door. When the deceased first arrive, they may only have it open a crack and confirmation from their living loved one is like saying "C'mon in!" and the door is open wide after that. The medium is not fishing as some may think, but merely looking for confirmation and a way to open the door.

My lesson in trust

I remember one occasion that this occurred

between myself and one of my clients, quite vividly. A young lady had come in to see me for a general reading. We sat together for a moment so that I could connect to her energy and I had her shuffle the cards that we were to use for her reading. Almost immediately, I felt that a deceased loved one had come in to see her.

I wasn't sure of the connection at first. So I just went with what I was seeing. I think that the most valuable tool that I have developed is to trust the information coming in and to only describe what I am seeing or experiencing. It is NOT my job to figure out the message. That is between the living and their deceased loved one.

In the past, I would try to figure out what the message is by taking in the information, processing it in my own mind and trying to describe what I *thought* the message meant to them. This is surely the WRONG way to communicate with the deceased for others and I can tell you firsthand that it is a recipe for disaster.

Here I am, describing what I am seeing to her. I see this child. The child is coming in so vividly that I can describe every fine detail, especially the long blonde curls. And to me, this child looks like a little girl because of these long blond curls.

Nothing else is coming through for me except for the visions of this child and a feeling that I am communicating with the father of this child. What I was doing (and what I didn't realize I was doing until after) was communicating only that I was seeing a child. In my mind, I thought that perhaps the child had passed and was trying to figure out who this child belonged to.

I was beginning to feel stuck in this vision and didn't want to continue to assume that her child had passed, even though I had suspected it. I then took a deep breath, brought my focus back to center to allow myself to experience the messages free from my own interpretations of them and asked the spirit that was attempting to communicate with me for clarification.

I saw the child again and then got the sense that the person communicating with me was a man, that this was their child together and that the woman sitting across from me was his wife.

I then just flat out asked her if the father of her child had passed, because he keeps showing me this child and I "feel" like he is the father. She got a little teary and confirmed that her husband had passed recently and that they had a child together, only it was a little boy (with long blonde curls) and not a girl as I had described.

As soon as I got confirmation from her that this was her husband, the door had opened, his energy got stronger and I was able to get more information from him.

He had recently passed from a tragedy and wanted to make sure that his wife and baby were OK. He also wanted to let her know that he was OK and was with them. He wanted her understand why this happened and to be able to have some closure.

I received a letter from her months later, thanking me for making this connection for her as it was the only way that she was able to get closure. She included a picture of her son so that I could see how accurate my description of him was and wanted me to know that she had previously been to numerous grief counselors to no avail. Had I not received verbal confirmation that this was her husband, we may not have gotten to the point where she was able to get the closure that she needed so much.

A message from nature

Sometimes confirmation will come after the reading, where the deceased will specifically describe something that their loved one will experience or see in the future, to let them know that they are with them.

These signs can range from seeing a specific plant or animal in an unusual place to finding hidden objects in the home.

I have noticed that this happens often and I believe this is because it is one of the easiest ways for the deceased to manipulate energy.

My cousin always sees deer nearby now that her husband transitioned into the spirit realm and swears that they are messages from him. The deer just stop and stare at her and will often times block the road that she is driving on. He has told me that he is sending them to let her know that he is nearby and has the ability to guide them in her direction

When making an attempt to communicate with the deceased, it is important to trust that the information coming in is real and true and to only

focus on what you are experiencing. Tell it like it is
– now that's a good phrase to read by.

Chapter 4
WHAT THEY WANT US TO KNOW

When we connect with a person in life, we connect with them on a soul level. Sometimes the connection can be so strong that it seems as if we know them intimately even though we have just met.

I believe that this occurs because our souls have met before and we are recognizing their spirit. Even though someone has left us in the physical world that soul level connection stays strong.

Our loved ones long to make a connection with us after their death as much as we do and in most cases for the same reasons.

But what do they want and why do they make

such an effort to communicate with us? What is so important that they feel the need to return to us in their spirit form. Based on my experience with making these connections and conveying messages to and from loved ones, I've come to realize that being deceased is really not much different than being alive except for the obvious lack of a physical body.

Even though the deceased are no longer confined to a physical body, or have to adhere to the rules that apply to life and living, that person's memory that they have of their life lives on. In fact, many of the deceased that I communicate with will also express the same personalities they had in life.

I have compiled a list of the most common reasons that the deceased will come forward during a reading with me and try to communicate with us...the living.

They want us to know that they are OK.

The most common message that I deliver to the living from their deceased loved one is "I am OK". They can sense when you are worried about this and need to let you know that they have made it safely into the spirit realm and that they are doing well. Most of the spirits that I have had the honor of connecting with are actually doing better than they were in life.

If someone was in physical pain during life, they want their loved one to know that they are now pain free in the spirit realm. If they were in emotional turmoil or had problems with their focus, they want their loved ones to know that their thoughts are clearer in the afterlife.

Physical ailments no longer keep their personal energy down and they are free to come and go as they please.

When the daughter of a good friend of mine passed away, she came to me within moments of her death. She was giddy with joy and filled with "Yippee" and "Yahoo" energy. Even though my friend had just lost her daughter and I knew that as a human, I was supposed to be sad for her I could not help but giggle with joy knowing that she was safe and in a good place.

She said to me "Michelle, this is so great! I can go anywhere now. Look how fast I can move!" she spoke as she shifted her energy to the left, right, up and down. She then said "Tell my Mom I'm OK and I'm so happy!"

She had been in a wheelchair for most of her life, yet you would never know that she had a disability. Her positive outlook and bubbly personality made this young lady lovable beyond belief. It's no wonder that she touched so many hearts when she was alive. She lived her life to the fullest of her physical ability and once her spirit was set free she was ecstatic. It was truly a delightful experience to witness her joy.

She came to me a few more times after that first visit. Each time filled with a joy that I wish I could bottle up and drink in. Even as I write her story, I can see her smiling spirit in my mind.

I didn't share my experience with her mother right away and instead decided to share it with her aunt so that someone could know that she was doing OK. I eventually delivered the message to her Mom when the time was right.

They want us to have closure

They also want to make sure that we are OK and that we have closure. Closure comes when the living can find a sense of peace around the loss of their loved one. Many people are afraid to find closure because they are afraid that this means they have to let go of their memories of their loved one and let go of them.

This is not the case, however, and I cannot put into words the positive impact that closure can bring to someone. Sometimes closure can come simply by knowing that your loved one is OK or knowing what happened during their final hours.

But for most, closure comes when we are able to forgive ourselves or our deceased loved one for the missed opportunities and unfinished business between us.

This is evident in the story of Rick. Rick had accidentally shot himself and came through to let his wife know that he was still by her side and looking out for her. She was one who never believed in spirit communication and was having a difficult time dealing with his death.

The night before I was to see her mother, he

came to visit me in spirit. He was insistent that I tell her about how he was at the beach and left three items for her to find and that he was sorry because it was supposed to be four. Strange message right? I could have tried to figure out what this meant, but the message was not for me. So when I saw her the next day, I delivered it as simply as it came.

Her eyes widened and before I knew it she was dialing her daughter's number on her cellphone. When her daughter picked up she told her to hold on, handed me the phone and said "Here...you tell Lisa what you just told me." I relayed the same message that her husband had given me the night before and she confirmed that she had recently walked the beach in his memory and found four shells in a row. The fourth one was broken, so she threw it back to the sea. She had told her mother that she thought that her husband left the other three for her neatly in a row for her to find so she kept them.

No one else knew about the shells but her and her Mother. When we finished the call, her mother informed me that she was grateful that her son-in-law had made contact since her daughter was having such a difficult time with moving on and that she had been worried about her.

After that call, Lisa agreed to a session with me to connect once more with her husband Rick. Obviously, he had more to say, she thought.

We scheduled a phone session for her about a week later. Since I had connected with her husband's energy before, I was able to make an immediate connection. He wanted her to know that he had been by her side the entire time looking out for her and her daughter.

He also wanted her to know that it was not her fault and that he's not really sure what happened except that he was extremely confused at the time and his thoughts were fuzzy. There was nothing she could have done differently and he would always love her and make sure that she was taken care of.

I then saw her with someone else and him happy for her. He worshiped her in life and wanted her to find someone who would take care of her, like he did. He assured her that he would continue to look out for her and left her with a specific sign to look for from him to signal that she should step back and slow down.

I was honored to experience and help facilitate closure for her. I hear now that she is pursuing new relationships and is finally able to heal knowing that her husband's death was not her fault.

They want to celebrate with us

Deceased loved ones will also show up in our lives for special occasions, accomplishments and celebrations. Throughout the years I have come to recognize specific symbols to represent these occasions.

I will see birthday candles or balloons to represent an upcoming birthday, a certificate to represent a graduation or a family gathering to represent a wedding or anniversary.

In real charades, the more you play the better you get at solving the clues and developing your personal "tells". Playing charades with the deceased is similar in that the more you communicate the better you will get at recognizing the signs that you will easily recognize as messages.

Not too long ago, I had the honor of getting to know an amazing family of a man who had passed unexpectedly. I first met his brother and sister-in-law at a local psychic fair. They came in together, looking to gain insight on a personal matter going on in their life at the time. We addressed the personal matter and as I moved on to read other areas of their life, their brother-in-law comes in from the spirit realm to say hello.

He keeps showing me this motorcycle and how busy these two have been "getting things ready". They knew immediately that it was him and had secretly hoped that he would come through to approve of their efforts to help out. They had been planning a bike run in his honor and had all of the details worked out. In fact, the run was planned for the following weekend and he wanted his family to know that he was honored that they were doing this for his wife and children and that he would be there.

I was able to convey his excitement about the upcoming event because he first showed me a motorcycle followed by more motorcycles. He was insistent on showing me this and I want to point out that he did not die in a motorcycle accident. He was merely interested in letting his loved ones know that he would be at the event and how happy he was that they honored him like that.

I have since met with his wife and his son and he has sent many messages of love to his entire family and always lets them know that he is there in spirit, celebrating life's most precious moments with them.

They want to offer their assistance

Sometimes the deceased will come forward to warn us, help us prepare for a difficult situation or to help with upcoming deaths for other loved ones.

A couple of months before my sister passed away, she went through a period of time where she would have strange dreams. When she would have these dreams she would come to me feeling confused and would ask me to help her decipher the dream.

One particular dream came from a deceased loved one. She dreamed that she and a friend (both living at the time) were running through what seemed to be some sort of war zone. Fire, brimstone and destruction surrounded them and they were running through the streets to escape it.

My sister and her friend had separated at some point in the dream and she found herself drawn to an old fashioned ice cream parlor. Mind you, this dream occurred in the early 1990's and old fashioned ice cream parlors were pretty much non-existent. The ice cream parlor was unaffected by the destruction going on around her so she ducked in to find safety.

There was only one person in the shop and it was one of her friends who had passed away a year earlier. He stood before her calmly drinking a Coca Cola. She asked him in this dream "Jason, what are you doing here?" and he responded "Not much...I'm just enjoying this Coca Cola". He remained calm almost oblivious to the destruction going on outside.

She then said "Yeah I can see that but aren't you dead?" he answered "Yep". She told me that her curiosity got the best of her and she asked him what it was like. He told her that it was pretty cool and that she would know soon enough. Then he was gone. The dream startled her enough to wake her up and keep her from falling back to sleep.

When she asked me what the dream meant, I told her that I thought maybe he just wanted to let her know that he was OK. I also told her that it sounded like she stepped through some type of energy vortex that brought her to this peaceful place (the ice cream shop) so that she could connect with him.

She died within a month of that dream and little did I know then that he was there to help prepare her for her transition into the spirit realm.

They want us to know they are still with us

Sometimes spirits will come through simply to say hi and to let you know that they are still around.

although this was not the case in my sisters dream, it is usually the case when a deceased loved one seems to drop in for no reason.

I have one young man that truly deserves an honorable mention in this book to confirm this for you. His name is Josh and I must say he is quite the character, showing up all the time for his family members just to say hi.

Here's his story -

Josh died unexpectedly as a passenger in a car accident. The only warning that we received to indicate that this was going to happen was a brief mention during a psychic reading for his mother that one of her son's would be "going away" soon and God/spirit wanted her to be prepared.

Not too long after his transition to the spirit realm, the family came to see me, looking for answers. It was the first time that I was to be blessed with his amazingly upbeat and optimistic personality as I had not had the opportunity to meet him when he was living. He wanted his family to know that he was doing fine, but was more concerned with his brother who was still in the hospital recovering from his injuries incurred by the same accident.

Josh stood vigil at his brother's side until he was released from the hospital. I suspect that there have been many instances where a recently deceased person will postpone their own transition for another, but for me this is the only time that I have witnessed it first hand.

The accident that lead to his transition to the

spirit realm was quite some time ago and I still occasionally see his Mom and Sis for readings. No matter what is going on in their lives Josh always comes in to let them know that he is with them through the good times, the bad times and most of the time just to say "What's up?"

Josh left his human form with truly no regrets because he lived his life to the fullest and I believe he gives the perfect example for all of us to live a mindful life.

As you can see, the messages that come through for my clients are always loving and healing when they come from a deceased loved one.

So what is going on when you would like to connect with a deceased loved one and they do not come forward to communicate with you? This question was presented to me by a client who had hoped to connect with her aunt on numerous occasions, since her transition to the spirit realm, with little success.

She had read somewhere that only deceased loved ones who cared deeply for you in life will come forward in death and assumed that this person didn't care for her as much as she thought she did.

I have found this to not necessarily be true and would like to address this question. With my clients, I have come to realize that there are some good reasons why a deceased loved one has not connected with you.

1.)Your loved one could be on the other line

When we transition into the spirit realm, the things that are important to us will adjust to fit our new environment. Notice that I said "things" and that this is not to be confused with the people that were in our life.

We take on new 'jobs" that are spiritual in nature. Jobs that include lending energy to a living person who is going through a tough time or helping them get ready for their transition.

Sometimes this can take years. Their personal guides will be close by during this time as well as previously deceased loved ones who had agreed to assist them.

Spirit energy does have the ability to be in more than one place at a time, but in this case I believe that all of their spiritual energy is lent to assist with the transition and this could be why they are currently unavailable to chat with you.

The best way to look at this is to imagine that they are on the line with someone else and cannot answer your call to communicate. It most certainly does not mean that they do not wish to make the connection or that they do not love you.

2.)They may have already begun their next life

I believe in past lives. This is in part because of personal experiences and also because of what I've experienced with my hypnosis clients. I have witnessed many people recall memories from other lifetimes with such detail that they couldn't possibly have made it up.

I also have tried to intentionally make contact with a deceased loved one on behalf of a living person, only to sense that their consciousness was not available because they had taken on another human form. The interesting thing is that I am able to pick up an extremely distant vibration of their energy and although it is not nearly enough to play charades with the deceased, it is usually enough to pick up some clues as to where, when and to whom they have been reborn.

In most cases, the spirit will stay with their "spirit clan" and choose to be reborn into the same family or close by in proximity.

3.)They may not be vibrating at the same frequency as you or the psychic that is communicating with them.

We vibrate at different frequencies – plain and simple. In death, we seem to stay in the frequency that we were at in life. In other words, it seems to me that spiritual enlightenment or spiritual growth mainly occurs for us when we are either in human form or with human assistance.

I'm not saying that ALL spiritual growth can only happen while we are human, but based on my understanding of it, our spirits use the energy of being human to *experience* a spiritual growth of some kind. It is why I believe we choose to have a human experience...to raise our spiritual vibration.

This is how I have come to understand it:

The human body acts as a generator for the spirit to grow and learn new ways to connect and interact. My theory can also explain why earthbound spirits will need the assistance of the living in order to transition to the light.

I have yet to interact with a spirit who's personal energy (or spirit energy) "feels different than it did the first time that I connected with their spirit form...unless they have been earthbound and assisted to the light. It is then, and only then that I am aware of a shift in their vibrational energy. Other than that, their spiritual vibration is always the same.

I have (and I'm sure you have as well) experienced and "felt" fluctuations of a person's spiritual or energetic vibration during life. Especially when they are working on their spirituality. Have you ever said to yourself or another about another person "They've changed"? If you have, be sure to check on your own spiritual vibration because this surely means that either you or they have shifted the spiritual vibration to a higher level.

If the deceased loved one that you are trying to connect with is either vibrating at a lower frequency than you or the reader (this usually only occurs when a spirit is earthbound), or vibrating at a much higher frequency (which is most often the case), you may have a difficult time making a connection.

In this case, raising your own personal vibration can help you connect with deceased loved ones who were previously unavailable and can also help prepare your own spirit for it's adventures to the afterlife. I will give you some tips on how to do this in a later chapter.

PLAYING CHARADES WITH THE DECEASED

Chapter 5
ALL ARE WELCOME TO PLAY

Anyone and everyone has the ability to connect and communicate with the deceased. When you are willing to release all doubts and fears around it, silent your mind and open your heart you too can play charades with them!

You have probably done it already without even being aware of it. Have you ever had a dream of a deceased loved one that was so real that it seemed as if you were really talking with them? Deceased loved ones will often come through to visit us in our dreams. These types of dreams will occur during the time of sleep that you are between a state of deep sleep and partly awake. When we are in this state of sleep, we are able to communicate with loved ones who have transitioned into the spirit realm.

Professional psychics are able to access this state of mind while they are in the "awake" state by learning how to adjust their awareness so that they are purposely tuned in.

You can also learn these techniques and learn how to develop your personal tools to help you connect with the deceased safely and with confidence while you are awake. While you are learning how to do this, think of it as if you are learning a new way to play charades. A way to play the game of charades by deciphering the images, feelings and gestures in your mind's eye.

You will use the images, thoughts, feelings and sounds that you receive to create a storyline of messages from deceased loved ones. As you see, hear or feel these abstract messages you'll begin to put them together so that they make sense. Keep a notebook to track your progress and your personal "tells" as you develop them and most importantly practice...practice...practice!

As you are learning, I would also like you to keep in mind that not everyone is able to see a vision in their mind's eye. This does not mean that they are unable to reach a meditative state or cannot communicate with the deceased. There are many psychics I know who do not have the gift of inner sight, yet they can describe what they are experiencing as if they were looking at a picture of it.

They do this by sensing, feeling or knowing. If

you notice that you are having a difficult time "seeing" the memory in your mind, try sensing, feeling or knowing it and if that works better for you, go with it!

This is a great way to help you understand the way you process different information;
Start by allowing yourself to experience the color Red. As you experience this color, notice if you are actually seeing the color Red in your mind, or if you feel the energy of Red, and so on. Try this with all of the primary colors. By the time you are finished, you'll have a good idea about the way that you process information.
Once you understand the way you process information, you are better able to visualize and this can help you greatly with distinguishing messages from the spirit realm from other types of inner dialog.
I have outlined some simple tips to help you build a comparison for yourself. If you are serious about communicating with the deceased, it is best to practice these exercises daily until you are comfortable distinguishing the information that you are receiving from the spirit realm and your own internal dialog. This will give you a good foundation to start your readings with.
Feel free to try these methods to see if they help you develop a keener sense as well.

Step 1 - Learn to read your own memories

Start by sitting quietly for a few minutes and

still your mind. Once you are feeling relaxed, think about an experience that you had in the past that you enjoy remembering. It's important at this point to be sure that (1) you are recalling a memory form your past and (2) you are the only one in the memory.

Now, everyone imagines things differently and this is your time to allow yourself to experience it the way that you imagine. Are you able to see a scene unfold before you as if you were looking at it from the outside or do you remember this experience as if you are inside of the you from the past?

You might be someone who cannot see the memory at all and instead you may "feel" your way through the memory so that you get a sense of what you are doing and that's OK. Use the method that you are most comfortable with.

Once you have really connected to this memory, you can allow yourself to really get into it. Know the colors of the experience, your feelings about it and anything else that makes this experience your own.

Got it? ...Great!

Step 2 - Learn to read another person's memory

It's now time for you to learn how to read another person's memory of something. Don't worry this task is simpler than you think.

To start, sit quietly like you did when you were learning to read your own memories and still your mind. Only this time, once you are feeling relaxed you'll want to recall a story that someone else told you recently.

Try to think of a story where the person telling it was the only one in the story and remember that story as you had imagined it in your mind when they were telling it to you. Allow yourself to experience all of the tiny details like colors, images and feelings – just as you did before.

Begin to compare your experiences with the experiences that you had when remembering your own past memory. I find it easiest and most important to note the differences between the two. Write down the differences in a notebook.

Step 3 - Learn to read a made up story

Imagining a made up story in your mind also helps you learn what your comparisons are. You'll want to do this the same way you remembered the others by sitting quietly and entering into a relaxed state.

Only this time, you will want to make up a story in your mind. It can be something completely fantastical or a movie that you watched. Have fun and get creative. Just be sure that you include something that could not possibly be true.

Step 4 - Build a comparison

Get in touch with how this scene looks, sounds and feels in your mind and as you did before, compare it to the other two experiences.

Remember, you are looking for the differences. Writing them down in a notebook is a great idea if you are a visual person. You can then use your notebook as a guide to follow when you are attempting to communicate with the deceased.

Here is an example of how I process my inner dialect;

My memories: I remember it as if I am there again and I am inside of the me from the past memory.

Another persons memory: I remember it as if I am an onlooker watching close up (on the outside).

Made-Up story: Looks similar to another persons story, but it is further away and not as bright in my mind.

As you can see, this makes it easy for me to determine if what I am seeing in my mind is my imagination (my memories & made up story) or a message from beyond (another person's memory).

Step 5 - Ask for confirmation

When you believe that you have successfully made a connection with the deceased, ask them to give you a sign that is easy for you to recognize. They will gladly give you one.

If you are practicing with a friend, ask the person that you are reading for if what you are seeing makes sense to them or if they know what the sign that you are seeing represents to them.

Write all of your experiences in your notebook or journal to use as a reference for future readings.

This is an important step in the process. Even though candles can represent an upcoming birthday for me, they may symbolize something completely different for you. Or you may not even see candles at all. Everyone's experience is different.

I was working a psychic fair in another town when a woman (who apparently was also a psychic) sat down with me for a reading. I saw something specific that represented a new relationship coming in to her life in the near future. She saw something completely different in the cards that were laid out in front of her and became quite irate with me.

She insisted that I must be "projecting" my own personal experiences into her reading and that I needed to work on that. She was so insistent in fact, that she came back to my table a few more times throughout the day, interrupting other readings that were going on. She really wanted to make sure that I knew I was projecting, instead of reading.

I am sharing this story with you, not because it

is a case of communicating with the deceased but because it is an example of how important it is to build a rapport with your intuition and "tells" that you and only you personally understand (It is also a helpful hint that you should never try to read yourself during someone else's reading for you).

You will recognize these tells when you are communicating with spirit as well as every time you do a psychic reading of any kind and you will use them to effectively relay the messages to your clients. As psychics we DO project. We take in information in signs and symbols that we personally understand to represent something for another. This is how the psychic connection works. My suggestion when you are met with a challenge like the one I just described is to trust that the message is right for that person or they would not be sitting with you in the first place. Do not allow yourself to get frazzled by it and do not attempt to change or alter the information to suit another person's need to control it.

This is why...The same woman came to see me at the same psychic fair a year later. She wanted me to know that her reading with me was the best reading she ever got. In fact, she spent most of her time sending people to see me throughout the rest of the day!

So if you'd like to fast-track your way to spirit communication ask for confirmation, learn your personal tells, use them to help you and TRUST that they are true.

Step 6 - Keep it simple

Be careful not to read too much into the messages or try to guess why you are seeing what you are seeing. The biggest mistake that I see people make (and that I have made myself in the past) when they are attempting to learn any type of psychic art is to read too much into what they are experiencing.

We are curious by nature and this could be one of the most difficult tasks for you to master when learning how to communicate with the deceased. You may see, hear or feel something and naturally want to figure out what it means so that you can convey a message to someone. Let's say, for example, that you see a football field in your mind's eye while attempting to make contact and that a football field has no significant meaning for you.

Your conscious mind will automatically search for reasons that you might see a football field. Reasons that could include; "He liked to play football." or "She enjoyed watching football." when in fact there are so many more possible reasons that a vision of a football field could be showing up for them. Things that may have no significant meaning to you at all, yet can carry a world of meaning for someone else.

So how do we get past this need to read more into what we are seeing? The answer is simple and always the same. *Tell them what you are seeing, hearing or feeling – plain and simple.*

Say something like; "I am seeing a football field now. The field is green and it looks like the players are wearing yellow and black. Does this have any significant meaning to you or your deceased loved one?" Or you could ask, "Why am I seeing a football field?" This method is great because you are asking for confirmation from both the living and the deceased that you have made contact with and are sure to find clarification from either of them.

You might be surprised to hear that a husband had proposed at the football game that you described or that she was always complaining that I watched too much football.

And I'm going to tell you another important thing to note. Once that connection is made by either the deceased or the person that you are reading for, the line of communication opens wide and the messages will begin to come in clearer. Conducting your readings in this manner will help you to create a more positive experience for everyone involved.

Step 7 - Keep a journal

Keep a journal or notebook so that you can easily track the messages that you get and mark the confirmations as they come in. This will help strengthen your connection to the energy and help you to build your library of "tells".

A notebook will also prove helpful for you to use a reference while you learn and grow your personal experiences.

Some people are really great at automatic writing and use a notebook to help them open up their connection with the deceased. Try to use this technique and see if it works for you as well!

Chapter 6
NEGATIVE SPIRIT ENERGY

I'm sure that you will agree that everyone vibrates at a different energetic frequency. This is most evident when you meet someone for the first time and it just doesn't feel right. You may not really have a good reason for feeling uncomfortable around this person, but you just seem to subconsciously sense that something is off.

I have noticed that people will not only have the same personalities in death but can also carry their personal energetic vibration.

Especially if the person transitioned into the spirit realm in an unhealthy way or did not leave behind their emotional attachments when they passed. This can come across as a negative spirit experience (also known as Dark Spirit Energy) when the person has not come to terms with their own death and for some reason or another is dealing with it in a negative way.

Negative Spirit Energy can be broken down into different types of energy within its description. For the purpose of this book, I will be focusing primarily on the energy that is created by the deceased that is of a lower spiritual vibration. Entities and negative energy that has been created in ways other than from a lower vibration of the spirit are another topic all together and perhaps someday I will write another book that covers this.

If for any reason you think that you might have come across any type of negative spirit energy, I strongly suggest that you close your psychic channel and seek a professional that is trained in dealing with it.

I do not suggest or encourage you to engage in communication with any of the negative energies or lower vibrational spirits, but I do feel that it is important to discuss so that you can recognize and protect yourself from them. It is for this reason that I decided to include this chapter in my book. Much like it is important to wash your hands when you come into contact with something dirty or wear gloves to protect your hands from something that can irritate our skin, it is also important to cleanse and protect your spirit from unhealthy energies.

I will go into more detail on how to protect yourself in order to prevent this from happening all together in the next chapter. For now, I'll focus on the different types of dark spirit energy so that you can easily recognize them and disconnect your channel as appropriate.

Just as there are different types of positive spirit energy like deceased loved ones & spirit guides; there are also different types of negative spirit energy. These energies can be categorized as Earth Bound Spirits, Dark Energy Beings and Spirit Attachments.

Earth Bound Spirits

An earthbound spirit is just as described. A human spirit that is stuck in the vibrational frequency of being alive. When physical death occurs, our spirit detaches from the body and transitions into the spirit realm. A person is usually in communication with the spirits of deceased loved ones long before the well-known "white light" experience happens.

They come in advance to help ease the shock of the ejection of the spirit and to guide the newly born spirit to the light. When the deceased show me this process, they tell me that it is compared to when the human body is born. There is someone (usually a Midwife or Doctor) to help with the transition from living in amniotic fluid to breathing air. In the case of assisting with the transition into spirit it is to assist the soul with transitioning from human functions (breathing air) to energetic interactions (breathing energy).

When a person is getting ready to transition they may begin to see their deceased loved ones as early as a few months before crossing over into the spirit realm. The deceased loved ones will show up in dreams most often and in cases where death is really close, they will see them standing nearby and as they looked when they were living.

There are times when the spirit is not willing to accept that it is ready to leave the body. For whatever reason. They may be ignoring the signs, or feel that they have unfinished business in the physical world so they hold on. They will ignore the deceased loved ones that are nearby and fight to stay in the human form.

In these cases their spirit will stay in the lower energetic vibration of earth when their body dies. Since there is no more physical body, their awareness can go into a type of shock keeping the spirit stuck and what many people call "earth bound"

When a spirit becomes earth bound, their vibrational level will stay in the lower vibrations of earth and have a difficult time transitioning to the higher vibrational realms of the spirit. When an earthbound spirit is present, you will experience a heavy feeling in the energy coming from them. You also might see the spirit as Black & White or Grey in color and experience a sense of sadness, anger or despair.

When a spirit has successfully transitioned, the feeling is light, uplifting, colorful and euphoric. Earth bound spirits will not be able to express this type of energy.

They often show themselves as apparitions of their human form that seem to appear at the place of their death, where they lived when they were alive or beside a loved one that they do not want to part from. They will also give off a "funky" energy that just doesn't seem right. Most hauntings are the result of earthbound spirits.

When they attempt to communicate with you, you will notice a few details that will stand out.

•When asked their name, they will most of the time give you a human name that belonged to them when they were living either from the most recent life, or a past life.

•When you attempt to connect with their energy, it will feel dense and uncomfortable. It will also be free from any color, vibrationally or visually.

•They always carry with them some sort of negative emotion that can range from Anger, Fear, Sadness, etc.

•They are able to produce physical manifestations of their emotion, i.e., broken glass, electrical surges, physical shadows, etc.

I believe that the negative experiences of my childhood were a result of earthbound spirits. I learned recently that an old man had died in the house before my parents purchased it. As I reflect on those experiences now, I can clearly see and understand his attachment to the house.

Like attracts like plain and simple – It's an energy thing and negative spirit energy is no exception. As the years passed and his home became run down (it had been empty for a long time), he attracted more lower vibrational energy into it and by the time, we moved in it was a playground for negativity.

In most cases you can help an earthbound spirit transition into the spirit realm or go to the light simply by telling them that you are not the light they seek and telling them to look up and go to that light instead.

When you have asked an earth bound spirit to transition and they refuse to leave or are causing problems in a home or the environment, it is time to call a professional that is trained in the area of Spirit Releasing, Soul Retrieval, or some other sort of ability that helps spirits cross over into the light.

Dark Energy Beings

Dark Energy Beings are different in that they are spiritual energy that has never experienced life as we experience it. They are the spirit entities of an extremely low vibration and sometimes can simply be the manifestation of hate, jealousy and fear.

Dark energy beings are more often than not, created by humans. Some are created purposely with the intention of malice, while others just simply manifest of their own accord as a result of negative emotions. The feeling that you will get from a dark energy being is an extremely low vibration that resonates at the vibrational frequency of a pure primal nature.

It is the energy that can be best compared to the that of a wild animal. It seeks merely to survive and feed and it is concerned only with its own existence.

Here are a few distinguishing signs that a dark energy being has made contact:

•When asked their name, they will oftentimes not give a name at all or provide an unusual non-human name like bealzabob, or similar.

•You will not have to (or want to for that matter) connect to their energy. They will gladly let you know that they are there and your body will respond with feelings of fear or an extreme headache in one spot.

•Their energy will also be quite strong and forceful.

•They can and will produce physical manifestations like banging on walls, slamming doors, black shadows either in physical form or out of the corners of your eyes, etc.

•They can induce headaches, especially in the area of the third eye (located just above the eyebrows in the center of the forehead).

If you happen to come across this type of energy when you are attempting to communicate with the deceased, or even if you suspect that it might be a dark energy being, close off your channel immediately and contact a professional who is trained in this field.

Dark Energy Beings can be sent to the light if done properly. In fact, most of the dark spirits that have been sent to the light become light energy beings whose main purpose is to assist other spirits with the transition from a lower energetic vibration into the higher spirit realms.

Spirit Attachments

Spirit attachment happens when either an earth bound spirit or a dark energy being attaches itself to a living persons energy.

We are spiritual beings inside of human bodies, and it is important to keep in mind that no matter how high we are able to raise our spiritual vibration, we are still surrounded by an earth bound shell. Our bodies keep us grounded as we work though the challenges of living a life and help us with the human experience but can also leave us open for spiritual attack and attachments, if we are not careful.

Even those of us who practice the utmost care in protecting and clearing our energy can find ourselves dealing with spirit attachments. Since an attachment involves a human host so to speak, it is best for me to outline the distinct signs of a spirit attachment based on responses from the person that they have attached themselves to.

•A person with a spirit attachment will not "feel" like themselves or will have shown signs of a new habit/belief that seems to come out of the blue.

•They will almost always be able to pinpoint an exact time frame when things shifted for the worst in their life.

•You (the psychic) may be able to see a dark spot in their aura, or feel that they have dark energy attached to them.

•They almost always manifest addictions and unhealthy emotions for their host.

More people have spirit attachments than we would think and if you come across this type of spirit energy, it is important to not only disconnect your energy from the person that you are doing the reading for but to also direct them to a professional that can help them remove the attachment.

It is also important for you to close your psychic channel and clear your own energy as soon as you are able. The reason for this is because when you open up your psychic energy for a reading, you are opening up your energetic field. I have had a few occasions where spirit attachments have attempted to come to my spiritual energy while reading for the person that they were attached to.

Negative Spirit Energy in the Home

When negative spirit energy is present in a dwelling it can affect everyone that comes in contact with it. This is especially true for family members who live in a home together that has some type of spirit attachment.

With the exception of places that have a well known haunting going on Negative spirit energy in a dwelling can oftentimes be overlooked. It also cannot be removed by simply smudging with sage.. The sage will temporarily dispel the energy, but unless it is properly cleared, will eventually return. Always have someone who is knowledgeable in house clearing come in and clear it for you or your client.

Some symptoms that are common with having negative energy in the home include:

•Constant arguments and angry outbursts between family members

•Lack of sleep for most of the family

•Unexplained electrical and appliance malfunctions

•Constant minor illnesses (colds, flu, etc.)

And in severe cases:

•Family Members may experience addiction problems

•Suicidal/Homicidal thoughts

•Serious Illnesses

These symptoms can also apply for a multitude of other reasons as well, so go with your instincts or the instincts of the inhabitants of the home. If you or they are feeling that this is the problem, schedule a house clearing for them.

PLAYING CHARADES WITH THE DECEASED

Chapter 7
PROTECTION & PREPARATION

When my siblings and I were dabbling with the Ouija board many years ago, we did everything wrong when it came to communicating with the deceased. We did not bother to (or know how to) protect our personal energies.

We were not interested in preparing the space where the connections were made, nor did we properly close off the connection when we were done and we left ourselves open for all the negative experiences that followed.

Did we cause all of those scary things to happen? No, we certainly did not – but it all could have been avoided had we been knowledgeable about what we were doing and been responsible about protecting ourselves and our personal energy.

It is my intention for writing this book that it helps you to have a positive experience when it comes to communicating with your deceased loved ones and the loved ones of others. This type of communication has the potential to be the most beautiful experience that you and the person you are reading for have ever encountered...and I truly want that for you.

If you can relate to my childhood stories of fear and terror, I also want you to know that your experience did not have to be that way either and by incorporating a simple ritual of protection and clearing, you can have a better experience for yourself in the future.

When planning to open up that channel and allowing yourself to communicate with the deceased it is important to learn first how to protect your own energy. It is also important to learn how to properly disconnect or close off the energy when you are finished.

For me, this is a constant practice. I have met and know some people who are able to open and close their psychic channel at will – I am not blessed with that option as my connection is always open, so I need to make sure that I am always protected. I find it easiest for me to perform both a morning and an evening ritual of clearing and protecting my personal energy before bed each night and in the morning before I do any psychic work. This ensures me that I am always protected and safe from picking up spiritual "junk".

Creating a daily ritual for yourself should be the first step that you take towards your protection and preparation practices. It is important to learn how to protect your personal energy at all times now that you have opened (or expanded) your channel of communication to the spirit realm. This is because as you open and expand your awareness, you will in turn be raising your vibrational frequency. This heightened vibration will continue to open and expand even when you are not actively communicating with the deceased.

Earlier, I spoke of spirit attachments and the different causes of them. It is not my intention to tell you about them to scare you in any way. I tell you about them because they are very real and also can be avoided. One of the easiest and most effective ways to avoid picking up a negative attachment is to develop your own daily regimen of clearing and protection.

I believe that keeping the spirit self cleansed and protected is as important as washing your hands daily. If you did not wash our hands on a daily basis, you'd leave yourself open to germs that could possibly bring illness or worse to your bodies.

When working in the spirit realm, it is possible that you will encounter some undesirable energies that could at the very least, make you uncomfortable. So it is just as important to learn to make it a habit of protecting and cleansing your energy throughout the day to help protect you from the germs of the spirit realm...Yuck!

In order to effectively communicate with the

spirit realm, we must let the spiritual energy touch our personal energy in some way. When we allow outside spiritual energy into our own energy, there will always be some sort of energetic residue left behind. Even if the spirits energy is of a higher vibration it will still leave a residue. After a while this residual energy can become stagnant and eventually leave you feeling tired and out of sorts.

Learning how to keep your personal energy clean and clear can be as easy as learning how to wash your hands and once you have done it for a while, you will begin to do it automatically. Here are some great suggestions that you can try to help keep your energy spic and span.

Keep your personal energetic vibration at the highest level possible.

The easiest way to do this is to spend time engaging in activities that make you happy. It is a proven fact that joy and happiness alone can raise your energetic vibration quickly and effectively.

People can tend to get caught up in the stereo typical belief that one must become a monk or spiritual guru of sorts in order to raise the spiritual vibration. This couldn't be further from the truth, and although spiritual techniques can (and do) help raise the energetic vibration considerably, it is not necessary.

Incorporating joy, laughter, song, dancing, meditation and unconditional love into your life will also help keep your personal energetic vibration high, thus protecting you from unwanted energies.

By allowing yourself to get caught up in feelings like fear, anger, jealousy and depression you leave yourself open to the negative energies that are nearby. Start today to make it a habit of recognizing when these feelings come to the surface and wash them away with the opposing, higher vibrational feelings of joy and love.

If you happen to "pick-up" some negative energy in spite of your efforts to avoid it, don't worry about it. You can easily recognize and clear it from your personal energy when you make it a practice to keep your energetic vibration raised. You'll get used to being in this type of energy to the point that you'll know right away when something is not quite right.

To clear the negative energy simply allow yourself to get in touch with the area that has been affected and fill it with white, cleansing light (or Reiki if you are attuned with it). You could also smudge yourself with Sage smoke or spritz.

If you have an energetic clearing method that works for you, use it. If not, I suggest that you research the many different methods available and adopt one that works for you.

***Make a statement that only those vibrating
at the same (or higher) level as you may connect***

with your energy.

When you make this statement on a regular basis, it will eventually become a belief for you that embeds itself into your subconscious and super-conscious minds. Once your subconscious has been programed it will automatically create an energetic barrier around your body that only allows energy in that is of similar or higher vibrational frequency as yours. When you do this, you may also notice that the people who are drawn into your life are on a similar spiritual path as you are. You will also begin to attract clientele that is in perfect alignment with the services that you provide (if you are a professional psychic).

When the statement becomes an integral part of your super-conscious or higher self, other energies recognize it and will respect it. I have found this to be quite effective in protecting my personal energy from unwanted visitors and have used it for many years.

It will work best for you when you say it aloud but you can also make the statement in your mind if you feel more comfortable.

Build a sacred shield around yourself

The method of protecting your personal energy by creating an energetic barrier around your body is known as "Shielding". Creating a shield is quick and easy to do. The simplest shield to put up around yourself is to imagine a protective bubble around yourself and that the bubble is impenetrable.

You can get as creative as you'd like when it comes to creating this bubble, just be sure that the circumference is a few feet out from your body and is surrounded by white (or protective) light. The light can come from anywhere that is sacred to you. Some suggestions include; God, The Universe, Spirit, from within yourself, the earth, etc. I have also known people to visualize symbols on the outside of their bubble, while others will fill the inside with a golden glow.

My personal shield is a spiral of white light that surrounds me and is impenetrable to all that do not have my permission to cross through. When I am setting my shield, I say aloud "I surround myself with spirals of light that none shall cross", while visualizing a white spiral of light coming from the earth.

Carry a protective gemstone

A good friend called me last week to ask my opinion on a tender subject that she had been dealing with in regards to her son. Apparently he had been experiencing nightly visits from a deceased person that was diligent in trying to communicate with him.

The problem became apparent to her after receiving a call from his school that he was in hysterics about this ordeal and claimed that the man had followed him to school. Mind you, the boy is nearly nine years old. A disturbing encounter at any age, but at nine you can expect him to share his experiences and fears openly at school. And he did.

She had called me for assurance that her son was in fact 'seeing' this ghost and wondered if he should see a counselor.

I told her that although I did feel that this was a case of the deceased attempting to make contact with him, it wouldn't hurt to follow through with a professional opinion for two reasons. 1. Just incase this was not a spirit and merely a case of minor hysteria (hey, it happens quite a bit at nine..trust me!) and 2. It never hurts to have a safe place (outside of family) for a young person to share such a frightening experience.

Then the conversation moved back to questions like "How did this happen?" and "How can it be remedied and avoided in the future. My first suggestion to her was that he shield himself by creating the protective bubble of light. Next I suggested that she have him carry a gemstone. Although I myself can be known to be what I like to call a gemstone junkie, I find that children respond the best to gemstone energy.

We discussed what might be the best stone for him to use. One that would bring protection from lower vibrational spirit energy and at the same time make him feel safe.

During a follow up call to her, I learned that although he is still experiencing the "visitors", they are at a distance and he feels protected from them.

You may have noticed that many professional

psychics will wear gemstone jewelry to activate and enhance their psychic connection. In fact, I do the same myself.

What you most likely will *not* notice is the protective gemstone tucked away in their pocket or around the neck. The one used to help them keep out the lower vibrational energies or to clear their energy when the connection is closed.

I have compiled a small list of some of my favorite protective and clearing gemstones for you to use as a reference. These will surely help you get started and if the qualities of a certain gemstone resonates with you, you can purchase any of them either online or at your local spiritual store. The vibrational qualities are the same whether you buy an individual stone or buy a piece of gemstone jewelry to wear.

If working with the energy of gemstones excites you, I suggest that you expand your knowledge of them and their spiritual qualities. A great tool for this is a book called "The Crystal Bible" by Judy Hall. I use it regularly myself and it is where I got some of the gemstone descriptions that I have listed here.

Selenite

Selenite has a translucent milky white color with a very high vibrational quality. It brings clarity of mind by opening the crown and higher crown chakras and accessing higher guidance and angelic consciousness.

Selenite can be used to form a protective grid

around the house or your psychic space that does not allow outside influences in by placing one in each corner of the room or your home. Selenite wands can be used to detach residual spiritual energy from the aura.

Selenite is a self clearing stone that also has the ability to clear other stones and objects from negative energies. I always keep a piece of Selenite with my psychic tools when they are not in use to keep them clear.

Black Tourmaline

All Tourmaline will cleanse, purify and transform dense energy into a lighter vibration. It grounds spiritual energy and will form a protective shield around the body.

Black Tourmaline, specifically protects against psychic attack, spells, ill wishing, and negative energies of all kinds.

Black Tourmaline works best at drawing off negative energies when it is placed to point outward from your body or your psychic work area.

Turquoise

Turquoise is a great dual purpose stone that can help enhance your psychic connection to the spirit realm as well as protect you from any negative energies.

Turquoise promotes spiritual attunement and enhances communication between the physical and spiritual worlds. Placed on the third eye, it enhances intuition and meditation.

Turquoise is also a purification stone. It dispels negative energy and clears electromagnetic smog.

Lapis

Lapis Lazuli is a protective stone that contacts spirit guardians. This stone recognizes psychic attack, blocks it,and returns the energy to its source.

Lapis Lazuli opens the third eye (commonly known as the energy center that controls psychic awareness), and balances the throat chakra (communication). It stimulates enlightenment and psychic abilities.

Lapis works best when worn as an amulet around the neck or carried in the pocket.

Malachite

Malachite is by far, my favorite gemstone. I keep it with me to help protect my energy even when I am not working with the spirit realm and I use it to help strengthen my psychic connection.

Malachite amplifies both positive and negative energies. It grounds spiritual energy into the planet which can prove helpful when working to remove spiritual residue. It is believed by some people, myself included, that Malachite is still evolving and will be one of the most important healing stones of the new millennium.

Malachite is an important protection stone because it absorbs negative energies and pollutants easily, picking them up from the atmosphere and the body.

Malachite should be cleared both before and

after use by placing it on a quartz cluster in the sun. Do not use salt to clear this stone as it will damage the surface.

Many years ago, people would carry this stone to protect from lightening and other natural disasters because it is believed that the stone will crack to warn of impending danger.

Whether you are working with gemstones to protect your energy or the tools that you will use for your psychic work, it is just as important to protect and clear them as it is yourself.

Here are some helpful tips to lead you in the right direction when it comes to blessing tools, keeping them clear of negative energy and setting up a protective area to work in;

Cleanse and bless your tools often

If you plan to (or currently) use tools like a pendulum, cards, candles or spirit board to connect with the spirit realm, you'll want to make sure that they are also protected, cleansed and blessed for use as tools for your divination purposes.

I create a sacred ritual around cleansing and blessing new tools that I use in my practice. You can do the same if you wish or simply follow some of the tips outlined here. There is no know-all tell-all, absolute way to do this. It is all in the intention of attracting only that which is of the light.

When I get a new tool that I will be using to

connect with the spirit world I cleanse it first with blessed water. My blessed water is made in advance by me and I keep it in a bottle so that it is readily available. To make this water, I mix some sea salt in water and bless it under the light of the full moon.

To cleanse my tools, I will place some of the water on a cloth and wipe down the item. Once it is cleansed, I hold it in my hands for a few minutes (or hold my hands over it in prayer) so that my energy is imprinted in the item. I then hold it up to the sky and "introduce it" to the universe as a tool for my divination. I ask that it be blessed with the highest and purest of light.

Some things that you can do to cleanse and bless your tools before using them to connect with the deceased are:

•Wash them with a blessed water.

•Smudge them with Sage, Sweet-grass or Palo Santo (holy wood).

•Clear & bless them with Reiki symbols.

•Create a sacred ritual with candles, etc.

When you use a physical item to connect with the deceased, it is important to also cleanse it when you are done. The reason for this is because, many times, the spirit realm will touch your tools with their energy while you are working with them. The energy will leave an imprint on the item. Even if the session is a positive experience, you'll want to cleanse your tool of this energy before putting it away.

You do not necessarily have to re-create the ritual that you used when you first blessed the item. A simple cleanse will do the trick. I simply smudge my tools with White Sage after each session.

It is also a good idea to keep a protective item near the tool when it is not in use. I like to keep shards of Selenite gemstones with all of my tools. Selenite is a gemstone that carries cleansing and protective properties. When I was younger, I kept a rosary with my Tarot deck to protect it from negative energies when it was not in use. When choosing your protective items, do what feels right for you!

Always prepare yourself and your space

When you prepare the space that you will be working in, you create an imaginary wall that will protect both you and your client from lower vibrational spirits and dark energy.

I have to say that this is the most important thing that you can do to prior to making a connection with the deceased. The spirit realm navigates by way of energy. When you open up your connection to communicate in this realm your personal energy will spread out from your body.

Sort of like a beacon that say's "we're open" to receive messages from the deceased.

Once you turn on (or up) the open light, the deceased will sense it and be drawn to it. Naturally they will want to come in to your sacred space and communicate. The protective walls that you create can act as a "members only" area that keeps unwanted energies out.

I am attuned to the Reiki energy. If you do not know what Reiki is, I suggest you do some research on it and decide if it is something that you'd like to become attuned in to use with your services. Reiki is a Japanese form of hands on healing that utilizes the flow of energy through the body.

Before I communicate with the deceased, I surround the area with protective Reiki symbols and then fill it with Reiki light. I have known others to do this as well. The most popular way to create a protective area is by using white candles that have been previously cleansed and blessed. If you have ever been to see a professional psychic you may have noticed that there are candles lit throughout the room around you. Most likely, the reader has set a protective boundary before you came.

Feel free to create your own ritual of setting your personal space as well. When we make things personal, we are able to add our own energy to them, making for a more positive experience. It is traditional to set your protective area by moving in a clockwise motion and breaking it down in a counter-clockwise motion.

I've created a diagram for you to use as an example. This diagram will work best if you draw out a similar diagram on a separate piece of paper that outlines the space that you will use to create your protective area.

Sample Room Diagram:

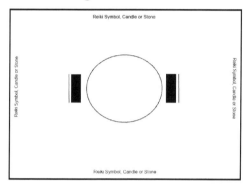

Here are some of the items/ideas that you can use to create a protective area for yourself.:

Option #1; *Surround your personal space with energy and fill it with white light.*

Start at the door or in a specific area of the room. (it is believed that the doorway to the spirit realm is in the East, so many people will start there). Walk in a clockwise motion around the room, stopping to face the center of each wall.

Each time you stop, say a prayer, call in your protective energy or place symbols in the air in front of you. As you walk to the next wall, you will be sealing the energy around you.

Once you have made it all the way around the room, you can imagine the area filling with white protective light. The room is now protected and sealed.

Option #2; *Set three or four candles around you or the area that you will be working in.*

If you have a specific room that you will use for communicating with the deceased it would be a good idea to purchase decorative candle holders that hang on the wall. They can be simple tea-light holders or as elaborate as fancy ones that hold the larger glass candles.

You'll want to purchase one for each wall in the room or at least enough to surround your sacred area. Try to place them as close to the center of the wall as possible. Also be sure to leave enough room at the top for safe fire burning.

Lighting the candles will activate the protective area that you have set. You'll want to light them in a similar manner as outlined in the previous chapter. Stopping at each candle and lighting it as you walk around the room in a clockwise manner.

Once all of the candles are lit, you can say a special prayer or imagine the area being filled with protective light and your space is protected and ready.

Option #3; *Gemstones can be set in a circle around you or one can be set in each corner of the room.*

Gather some "special" stones from nature or purchase ones from a spiritual shop that carry protective qualities.

When you are ready to set your protective space for spirit communication, follow the same manner as outlined before leaving a gemstone in each corner of the room. Gemstones can also be set in a circle on the floor around the area that you will be using to make your connection. I suggest that you only use this method when making connections for yourself however, as having a client step over the gemstones could be a tripping hazard and we want the experience to be as positive as possible when working with others.

Option #4; A pendulum can be used to create a spiral of light that spreads out and fills the room/space that you will be making a connection in. The outer edge of the spiral becomes the protective wall.

This is one of my favorite methods to use when I do readings in another person's home or for a private party. It is a quick and simple technique that takes little time. Not to mention it is quite effective.

To do this, sit quietly for a minute or two to get in touch with the pendulum's energy. Instruct the pendulum to set a protective circle around you and the area that you will be using to connect with the spirit realm.

Your pendulum will develop its own unique pattern that lets you know when it has started and when the area is protected and sealed. My pendulum will begin to spiral out from a tiny clockwise circle and will stop when it is complete.

It may take some time for you to master this technique. Especially if you have never worked with a pendulum before. I recommend that you at least try it once to learn if it is an acceptable method for you to use.

These are only a few of the many ways that you can prepare your space to create a protective barrier between yourself, your client and unwanted energies. Practice and experiment until you find one that works for you and once you find it, stick with it. You'll find that the more you use a specific technique the stronger it becomes and the quicker it takes to activate.

PLAYING CHARADES WITH THE DECEASED

Chapter 8
TOOLS OF THE TRADE

Now that you have an idea of the way that you personally communicate with the deceased, have developed some tools that you can use to make that connection stronger and have developed a way to protect your personal energy let's talk about the methods that you can use to communicate with the deceased.

Note that all of the methods described here can be used to help you open up your channel to the spirit realm. Use the one or one's that resonate with you most. However, I do recommend that you at least try each one out to see if it fits your personal way of communicating. Some of them can be lots of fun when done correctly.

No matter which of these methods you decide to try out, I have created an easy to follow outline in chapter nine to ensure that all of your experiences are fun and safe. I wouldn't want you to risk having the same negative experiences that my siblings and I experienced when we were children.

It is also important to note that by using any of these methods, you are in fact opening up and accessing channeled information from the deceased. These tools will certainly open up that channel, but once a connection is made, no matter what tool you use to get there, you are channeling that information into your psyche and translating through your human body. I want to make this absolutely clear so that you are aware of the process and can respect it.

Some people are not comfortable with the word "channel" as it evokes an often misunderstood images of where a spirit takes over a poor unsuspecting human soul. This is certainly not the case, when you are communicating with the spirit realm, but it is still important to be careful. You are allowing spirit consciousness to use you as a channel to communicate.

This IS channeling.

This reminds me of a time when I was putting together an event for a local psychic center. I helped with the advertising of an event for the store owner and had been putting together the finishing touches for the flier. In the advertisement, I had used the word "channel". I thought it fitting since the person who would be hosting the event was a known Trance Channel in the area.

Upon final review of the information that was to be published, the owner took me aside and said *"Michelle you have to remove the word "Channel" from the advertisement. It is a word that might be frightening for people who would have attended, if the word had been removed."* I was stumped. It took me quite some time to figure out how to advertise a Trance Channel without actually using the word "Channel", but I did and the store owner was happy.

What is it about that one word, that frightens people so much? I thought to myself...and I thought...and thought some more.

Finally here we are, addressing the same subject in a different light. This experience has led me to believe that it doesn't really matter what you call it in order for it to feel OK for you to do it. What truly matters is that you accept the fact that spirits who communicate with you in this manner can and will enter into your consciousness and use you to help channel their information. It is also important that you allow yourself to be made aware of any fears that you may have created around the subject and let go of them. Once this is done a clear channel will open for you.

I thought it fitting to start with the ouija/spirit board, since this was the first tool that I used (besides myself) to open up the channel of communication with the deceased.

In my experience this tool can be the most tempting one to try and at the same time the most frightening. As with all of the tools outlined here, It is my intention to lift the veil and allow you to see them in a new light. When trying them out, be sure to follow the outline that I have set up for you in chapter nine, properly protect yourself, be respectful of the energy and most of all have fun.

Ouija Board/Spirit Board

The Ouija Board or Spirit Board as it is called nowadays has really gotten a bad rap over the years. I believe that this is mainly because of the commercialization of it in the late seventies and early eighties. If you were a child during this time-frame and were fortunate... ahem...or unfortunate enough to have played with the popular Game by Hasbro "Ouija", I'm sure you know what I mean.

Many children, myself and my siblings included would eagerly anticipate messages from beyond with this supposedly easy to use game. The instructions would (and I believe still do) direct the players to wipe the board off to remove dust, sit in a dimly lit room across from each other place a couple of fingers on the pointer, focus and ask your questions one at a time. It is promised that once the questions are asked the pointer will begin to magically move around the board to highlight and spell out the answers to the questions you posed.

That's it! That's basically all that the

instructions indicate that you need to do to connect with the mysterious realm of the psyche. What would happen in most cases, as did with myself and my siblings as well as countless other people that I have had the opportunity to talk with about it, is that the intention created would open up some sort of porthole (for lack of better word) to the spirit realm. Unprotected and inexperienced people would inadvertently invite anyone in the spirit realm that was nearby and available to talk with. Lower Vibrational energy....higher....this did not matter. Well, you get the picture.

The reality of this little gem is that the Ouija board, when used properly is really one of the easiest ways for the deceased to communicate with us. Think of it from the perspective of the deceased.

Here you are, in the spirit realm. You still have conscious awareness and memories of your life. You are able to recognize the energy of your loved ones who are still among the living and you would like to communicate with them. Yet you no longer have a body to do this with. You are not easily able to tap them on the shoulder with your finger or use vocal chords to speak to them. You are able to manipulate energy, however, and have the ability to enter into their psyche.

When your living relative is able to quiet the conscious chatter of the world of the physical and focus inward. You attempt to connect with them but in most cases your messages are dismissed as imagination.

Spirits find it quite easy to manipulate the Ouija/Spirit board. They communicate through the psyche of the living people who are controlling the pointer and help them to subconsciously move it in the direction of the letters and numbers to spell out what it is that they are trying to say.

You must be connecting the dots right now and may be thinking to yourself. *Hey...wait a minute she just told me that when I am using a Ouija Board to communicate with the deceased, I am the one moving the pointer?* My response is yeppers, you sure are! Well, most of the time anyways. A spirit must use a lot of energy to move an object and most won't do it unless it is extremely necessary.

When manipulating energy, even the deceased know that energy sent out, will naturally follow the path of least resistance. Thus, a live person, in a meditative state sitting at a board with numbers and letters on it, while holding their fingers on a tool that easily slides across the board, is like a gift from the gods for them and they WILL use it and you to communicate.

Here's how to do it safely and effectively:

First prepare and bless your board as outlined in the previous chapter. You can use a board that you have purchased or make a homemade one.

When you are not using your board, keep it stored with a protective gemstone in the box. Be sure to clear the energy with sage or prayers both before and after using it.

When you are ready to use the board to connect with the deceased place it in the middle of the room or the area where you will be communicating, before you set the protective energy for the psychic activity. You'll want to do this so that the board is sealed inside the protected area.

When you are ready to begin, take a few slow deep breaths or use whatever method you have developed to bring yourself into a light meditative state and open up your psychic channel.

The board will work better if you have someone else with you but it is not necessary. Some people believe that it is unsafe to use a Ouija/Spirit board on your own. I do not find this to be the case as long as you have made sure to properly protect yourself and your space. I also recommend that you designate someone to write out the questions and answers as they come up or to record the session. It is most common to forget the messages that are given while communicating with the spirit realm. When you are ready to begin, follow this simple outline:

1.Place the pointer in the center of the board.

2.Rest the index and middle finger of each hand lightly along the edge of the pointer. You can either ask if there is a deceased spirit nearby that would like to communicate or ask to communicate with a specific spirit. When attempting to communicate with a specific spirit, it is advised to have either a photo of them nearby or an item that they once possessed. This will help them to recognize their personal energy and draw them towards the board.

3.After a while, the pointer will begin to move over to yes on the board, to signify that someone from the spirit realm has made a connection. This can take up to a few minutes so be patient. It can take the spiritual energy a few minutes to align and adjust to yours.

4.Once you have confirmation that a spirit is present you can proceed to ask more specific questions and watch as the answers are spelled out on the board for you.

Facilitating A Seance

If I were to describe my idea of what would be involved in conducting seance during my younger days, I'd have surely described a group of people sitting in a circle around a small round table each resting a couple of fingers on is edge. I'd have explained that as you ask the questions of the deceased that the table would tip in one direction or another signifying spirit activity.

While table tipping is certainly one way to conduct a seance, I have learned over the years, that this way is only one of many and if I were to suggest one method to communicate with the deceased as a group, I would not suggest table tipping be used for your first attempt. Not because it is ineffective, but because when we look at spiritual energy and how much skill it takes for a spirit to transfer their energy in a way that can physically move such a large object with the combined energy of only a few fingers of the living, we can safely assume that in order for a spirit to communicate with us by transferring enough energy to tip a table, said spirit would have to be skilled.

A skilled spirit has been able to make several successful connections by way of moving physical matter and if it is your intent to say hello to grand-mom and grand-pop, your attempts to communicate will more than likely go unanswered.

For best results, start small by using a lit candle in the center of the table or an upside down shot glass and instruct the nearby deceased to attempt to tip the glass as it sits lightly under your fingers or to move the direction of the flame's flicker. With practice you'll notice that one specific item will work best for you or the individual spirits that you are communicating with.

No matter what psychical items you will use for your seance (or if you decide not to use anything at all), here are the basic techniques to communicate with the deceased, using the tools that I have found to work best.

1.Sit in a circle with three or more people.

Although a seance can be performed with as few as one person, I find that three or more people produce the best results.

2.Enter into a light meditative state by taking three deep breaths together as a group, saying an opening prayer or using whatever method to open up your psychic channel that works best for you.

3.Start the seance by asking if there is a spirit present that would like to communicate with you. You can ask them to make themselves known by making a sound in the room, moving something or doing something else to let you know that they are there. I find this will work best with a lit candle in the center of the table and asking them to move the flame or put the candle out.

4.Once you are sure that you have made a connection with a deceased spirit that would like to communicate with you, you can begin to ask more specific questions.

5.You can use an item in the room or the preferred method that the spirit has used to let you know that they are there. For example, if the spirit has made a knocking sound to let you know that they are there, or made a candle flicker, you can build upon that to get answers.

6.You can then ask them to make a knocking sound if the answer to your question is yes, or move the candle flame to the left for yes and to the right for no.

7.When conducting a seance, be creative and maintain an open mind as anything can happen!

* Note: When working with candles to connect with the deceased, it is important for you to sit far enough from the candle as not to disturb the direction of the flame with your breath and to take note of any drafts in the room that may also affect the flame's flicker prior to conducting your séance.

The Pendulum

The Pendulum is a great method to use for those who would like to communicate with the deceased on your own. Pendulums are best known as a divination tool that is used to douse for water, find lost objects and answer simple yes or no questions.

The pendulum can also be used as a communication tool between you and the deceased. The way this works is similar to the Ouija/Spirit board in that the deceased will enter your higher consciousness to facilitate the movement of the pendulum.

Pendulums move as a result of tiny muscle responses in the fingertips. These responses are so minute that we are unable to feel them on a conscious level. With practice, the pendulum can become one of your most valuable psychic tools.

Before using a pendulum, you'll want to make sure that you are working with one that resonates with your personal energy. Once you find one, you'll also want to program it so that it will be an accurate assistant for you.

I have many pendulums to aid and assist me in my psychic work and each one is programmed to help me with a specific psychic task. I have a few that I use to open up my psychic channel before doing any psychic work, some that I use for healing and clearing energy buildup and some for communicating with the deceased.

If you decide to use a pendulum to communicate with the deceased, I suggest that you designate one for that purpose and use it only for communicating. The more you use it, the stronger the responses will be and it can eventually become one of your most used tools.

Selecting the pendulum that is right for you:

Take your time when looking for the right pendulum to use for your communication tool to the spirit realm. I've known some people to take up to a year in finding the right one.

You can make one by using a weighted object hung from a string, if you'd like, but I think you'll find that the pendulums available today are fairly inexpensive and beautifully made. Before you set out in search of the perfect pendulum be sure to make a statement to yourself (and the universe) that you are in search of this tool. This will ensure that spirit puts you at the right place and at the right time to find the perfect one.

While out and about, you may find yourself drawn to a specific pendulum. Usually we are drawn to the aesthetic appearance of it first...but trust me when I say that it is much more than that!

Pick up the pendulum and hold it in your hands to see how it feels to you. Is there a connection? If so, hold the end of the pendulum between your pointer finger and thumb so that the weighted end of the pendulum is hanging at the bottom and can swing freely.

Ask either out loud or quietly in your mind for the pendulum to show you 'yes'. Be patient and watch as it begins to move. The pendulum will respond differently for each of us and the combinations of movements can vary greatly from person to person, so don't be discouraged if your friends pendulum moves one way for yes and yours another.

It is for this reason that I recommend that you do not purchase a pendulum mat to use as they are designed with the creators methods of divination in mind and can tend to hinder the learning process for you if your YES/NO answers flow in a different direction than the direction outlined on the mat.

Once you are confident with the representation of a yes answer, go ahead and ask it to show you no. You will now be able to ask the pendulum things like; "are you the pendulum for me?", or "Will you make a good tool for me to connect with the deceased?", etc. Yes answers to these questions will indicate that you have selected well and have found your pendulum!

If you get a 'no' answer for any of the previous questions, or the pendulum is unresponsive, simply repeat the process with another one. Continue with this process until you find the pendulum that is right for you.

Activating and clearing your new pendulum

When you have found the right pendulum to work with for communicating with the deceased, you'll want to activate it for this purpose.

The method for activating and clearing pendulums is a little different than the method outlined in the beginning of this chapter. You'll definitely want to bless and activate it as a tool for your psychic activity, but when it comes to pendulums, this task is much easier.

Pendulums are self clearing in that they do not require smudging or salt baths to clear them before and after use. To clear a pendulum, simply hold the pendulum as you would for reading/communicating and instruct the pendulum to clear itself of any residual energy. Mine moves in a counterclockwise manner when clearing energy.

You can also use this method to clear a room both before and after using it for communicating with the deceased. More on that later.

Using your pendulum to communicate

There are two ways that you can use the pendulum to communicate with the deceased. The first and probably easiest way is to simply ask questions of the deceased that require a yes or no answer.

I recommend using this method when you are just starting out. It will help build up your personal connection with your pendulum quickly and provide accurate answers from beyond.

The second and more advanced way to communicate with the deceased by way of pendulum is to use a handmade chart or Ouija/Spirit board.

The chart or board will contain both letters and numbers that the deceased can point to in answer to your questions. Here is an outline on how to use a pendulum with a chart or Ouija/Spirit board.

1. Hold the pendulum in your hand and dangle it over the Ouija/Spirit board or chart that you have created.

2. Take a few slow deep breaths, or use the method that you have developed to open up your psychic channel.

3. You may notice that the pendulum will begin to move as your psychic connection is opening and expanding. (For example, when I use the pendulum to make a connection, my pendulum will spin in a clockwise circle as my psychic awareness is opening and expanding.)

4. When you are confident that your psychic channel has been opened, hold the pendulum over the board or chart that you have made and ask if there is a deceased spirit nearby that would like to communicate with you or ask to communicate with a specific spirit.

5.The pendulum will begin to move again and will eventually point to the yes area of the chart or signify a yes answer to confirm that there is spiritual energy nearby that wishes to communicate with you.

6.Once you have confirmation, you can proceed to ask more specific questions and watch as the answers are spelled out for you.

Directly Channeling Information

Although you will want to use what you know about the game of charades when communicating with the deceased for all of the methods described here, Channeling or Mediumship is most like playing charades than any of the other methods outlined.

When the deceased communicate with us in this way, the only tool that is required to open up the channel of communication is the mind. The deceased will send visual images, feelings and brief words that outline what they are attempting to communicate to us.

It is the job of the channel to properly translate the messages into viable information.

When it comes to channeling, there are two types that I think are important to discuss. The first and probably most well known is called trance channeling.

Trance Channeling occurs when a living person gives permission for a spirit to step into the person's spiritual self and take over for awhile, gaining access to that persons physical body. In order for this to happen, the living person will enter a trance state and the spirit will then step in and use the living person's body to communicate with others.

Spirits that are able to do this are usually highly evolved and in most cases, have never lived on earth or had a human form. If you are interested in learning more about Trance Channeling, I suggest you take a class on the subject since this method requires a lot of training and there are several rules to follow that will ensure your safety.

The second method is by way of reading channeled information from the spirit realm and is also known as mediumship. It is the one that I use most often when communicating with the deceased.

Activating the ability to read channeled information requires for you to first and foremost be able to truly let go of the fears that are associated with blocking a clear channel of information. Some of those fears can include the stigma that is associated with being a channel or medium as I discussed earlier.

Once that channel is open, you will be able to see images that have been sent to your consciousness from the deceased, hear messages and feel things to help you translate the information.

To ensure a safe and fun experience, follow this

outline that I have prepared for you.

1.Sit quietly for a moment or two, take a few slow deep breaths or use whatever method that you are comfortable with for opening up your psychic channel.

2.Allow yourself to become aware of the subtle energies that are around you and ask if there is anyone in the spirit realm that would like to communicate with you.

3.When the channeled information begins to come in through your consciousness, it will look, sound and feel different than your own   process. This is how you will know that you have made a connection.

4.Once you are confident that you have connected with a deceased spirit, you can begin to ask questions, or start a dialogue with them by speaking to them through your thoughts.

Psychometry

I love using Psychometry when communicating with the deceased and I highly recommend it to anyone just starting out with spirit communication. It is by far the easiest way to get started.

Psychometry is the art of holding an object and reading the memories of the spiritual energies that are attached to it.

For the purpose of spirit communication, it is best to use an item that belonged to someone who has since crossed over into the spirit realm. I recommend trying it first with items that belonged to someone that you do not know. Ask a friend to bring something like a piece of jewelry or favorite object of a deceased loved one for you to read. You can then describe what you are "picking up" from the item to your friend and test your accuracy.

I will oftentimes carry an earring from my sisters high-school prom with me. Whenever I come across someone who is just starting out on their journey of communicating with the deceased, I take it out and ask them to hold it for a moment, and tell me what they sense from it.

Almost everyone that touches it, sees or senses that it belonged to someone with dark hair and brown eyes and that it belonged to a family member of mine. When I tell them that it was my sister, most will say that they sensed or felt that also, but did not say because of my blond hair and blue eyes, it did not make sense to them that she could be my sister and they were afraid they'd be wrong.

When reading objects, or communicating with the deceased in any way for that matter, it is so important to say what you see, hear and feel. It really is that simple. Who knows, you may just happen to be reading for the only fair skinned, fair haired, blue eyed woman in a brown haired Italian family!

Here's how it's done:

1.Set a protective area around yourself or the area that you'll be reading in.

2.Take a few slow deep breaths to clear your mind. You may also use whatever method that works for you to open up your psychic connection.

3.Pick up the item and hold it with both hands. If the item is small enough, I like to cup it in my hands with one atop the other.

4.Allow information to flow from the item, into your spiritual consciousness.

5.Remember that the images, sounds and feelings that come from the spiritual memory of an object will come to your consciousness that same way that spirit messages will come – as an abstract image, sound or feeling.

6.Most importantly, trust what you are getting for information and do your best not to doctor it up with your own perceptions.

Automatic Writing

Automatic writing is just as it sounds. It's the psychic practice of writing (or drawing) on a piece of paper, free of conscious thought and allowing the super-conscious or higher self to write for you.

Those who have an artistic talent can even take it up a notch by turning the automatic scribbles into art. If you've ever seen a spiritual artist at work, you know what I mean. They seem to be lost in the moment and their hands will glide with the flow of energy as it creates an image of a deceased loved one or spirit guide through them.

Automatic writing can also be used as a means to open up the psychic channel, using the scribbles as a way to access the place in their mind where the spirit connection is made. To determine if automatic writing is for you, follow this simple outline.

1.Place a notebook or piece of paper in front of you on a table. Have a pen, pencil or paint brush in your hand as if you are ready to write or draw something.

2.Sit quietly for a few moments and focus on listening to your inner self.

3.Close your eyes (or keep them open if you prefer) and begin to scribble on the paper in front of you by making slow circular movements.

4.If Automatic writing is for you one of three things will happen.

> a. You will see actual words or images written on the paper when you are finished.
> b. You will begin to connect with the spirit

realm and receive messages from there.

c. You will draw an image of an angel, spirit or guide.

Tarot Cards/Playing Cards/Oracle Cards

The very cards you use for psychic readings can also be used to communicate with the deceased or to help open up your psychic channel.

I will usually use mine when a client asks to connect with a specific deceased loved one during a reading or asks if there is anyone around them that would like to communicate. It is much easier for me to toggle from psychic readings to communicating with the deceased, when I use this method.

I will often take the cards into my own hands towards the close of a reading and begin to shuffle them myself. This allows me to absorb the energy that the person I am reading for had left in them during their shuffle. I find that by connecting in this way, I open up the channel to the energy of their super-conscious. I then can access an open channel to any deceased loved ones that may wish to communicate with them.

Another way that I use the cards to communicate with the deceased is to layout five cards on a row, after meditating on the first name of a specific loved one that my client would like to connect with.

If their loved one is available and would like to

communicate with them, they will use the cards to communicate their message. This also works as a great opener for the psychic channel as well.

As you can see, there are many methods that you can implement that will help you to open up your psychic channel and communicate with the deceased. Keep in mind that all of these methods take practice and as your psychic channel gets stronger, you'll notice that you will no longer need to use any method other than your own mind to connect and communicate with the deceased.

Although it can be fun to continue with using the methods that you are most comfortable with!

Chapter 9
ARE YOU READY TO PLAY?

Are you ready to get serious and play charades with the deceased? I find that knowing the rules and having a structure or outline to follow on how to play is important while learning any game and charades with the deceased is no exception.

In this chapter I will cover the basic outline for you to use when first starting out. As you become more confident, you can tailor this outline to suite your needs as a psychic medium.

Before you begin, decide which tools you will be using to communicate and the type of reading that you will do. I've created a checklist for you to use as you follow the steps outlined here. I suggest that you write the checklist down in your notebook or journal and fill in the blank areas as you work your way through the chapter.

Checklist (use as your personal outline)

■The type of reading that you'll be doing:

○ Communicating on your own

○ Professional reading

○ Gallery style reading

■Method of creating protective barrier:

○ Positive energy barrier

○ Barrier of candles

○ Barrier of gemstones

○ Using the pendulum

○ Other

■Method of opening your psychic channel:

■The tools you will use to communicate:

○ Ouija/Spirit board

○ Seance

○ Pendulum

○ Directly channeling information

○ Psychometry

○ Automatic writing

○ Tarot/playing/oracle cards

■Method of closing your psychic channel:

■How will you cleanse and clear your personal energy, psychic space and tools.

○ Reiki

○ The pendulum

○ White light

○ Other

This is a great place in the book to stop, write down the checklist in your journal or notebook and take a short break if you'd like. When you return, you can follow this guide to easily outline your first game of charades with the deceased!

Playing Charades With The Deceased
Instructions/Outline

Object of the game:

To make a connection with the spirit realm so that you can communicate with the deceased in order to find closure, guidance, spiritual healing or to receive other important messages for yourself and others.

Number of players:

A minimum of two players is required (one living and one deceased), however this game can also be played as a group with an unlimited amount of players (both living and deceased.). Trust me when I tell you that the spirit realm does not respect or understand the meaning of the word "maximum capacity"

The deceased learn to play nice

George was a conservative, Christian college and high school professor. I had only met him a few times before his death but he was a great friend and mentor to my husband. It wasn't until about a year

*after his death, that we were able to communicate
with him again.*

*A group of us got together to help another
friend facilitate the "Everybody's psychic" weekend
at All world Acres in Lakeland, Fl. My friend,
Ashley, hosted the event. She put together a great
line-up of classes and workshops for the guests to
attend and one of them was a Saturday evening
group séance.*

*The Ouija Board was the tool that we used that
night and we were able to communicate with many
spirits of deceased loved ones through it. There
were so many of us there, that we broke up into two
groups, each with their own board to communicate
with There was one point in the evening on our
board that the spirit visitors got a little clogged up.
You see, there were so many that wanted to
communicate that their energies had merged into
one giant mass of mismatched messages.*

*George was one of the deceased in the mix who
was attempting to communicate with us. In fact, the
major power struggle was between him and the
other spirits who were attempting to run the board!*

*Talk about maximum capacity. He pretty much
blocked everyone else's messages due to his
urgency to be first. We eventually had to ditch the
board and focus on communicating directly with
the deceased so that we could determine who was
who. Also, I am sure that while my husband was
sitting at the board, George would not back down
or let anyone talk until he had his say.*

*I stepped outside for a breather and was able
to talk to George one-on-one. He had an urgent*

message for my husband, that I delivered to him in private and when I was done, his spirit backed off a little.

The deceased were not very cooperative with the Ouija Board for the rest of the night, but we had a great time until then. Just like in life when dealing with a bunch of people that all want to talk at the same time, it's best to walk away and plan to communicate another day.

Set up:
Whether you will be communicating on your own or with a group, you'll want to follow the same outline for setting up.

1.Decide which methods/tools that you will be using. If you have not done so already, cleanse and activate your psychic tools.

2.Choose the area where you will be working in and make sure it is an area where you will not be disturbed. Cleanse and clear the area.

3.Cleanse and clear yourself, by smudging, saying a prayer or using the method that you are most comfortable with.

4.Place any tools that you will be using to communicate inside the area that you will be working in. Usually a table works best for this.

5.Create a protective barrier around yourself, your tool(s) and the area.

Playing the game:

Once the space is prepared and ready, you may begin the process of opening and expanding your psychic channel. You can do this using the method that you are most comfortable with.

For me, the pendulum works best. I will sit for a moment and hold the pendulum in my hand so that it hangs just above my lap. I then imagine that I am opening all of my energy centers, starting with my root chakra and working my way up. The pendulum will move in a clockwise circle that expands outward as each chakra opens. I say a prayer while I do this. My prayer goes something like this:

I ask that all of my energetic channels be open for my psychic work today.
That I may stay grounded and focused.
(my root chakra).
That I remain passionate about what I do.
(my sacral chakra).
That I am fearless as I access the unknown.
(my solar plexus).
That I am able to both give and receive unconditional love.
(my heart chakra).
That I speak the truth and that the messages are clear and understood.
(my throat chakra).

That I am able to see the unseen.
(my third eye chakra)
That my messages come only from the purest of
divine light.
(my crown chakra)

You can develop your own method to open up your psychic channel, or use mine for now. Once your psychic channel is open and protected, you are ready to safely play the game of Charades with the deceased!

I have put together some basic outlines for you to follow whether you are communicating on your own, giving a reading for someone else, or giving a gallery reading for a group.

These are only a few suggestions based on what I found to work best for me and it is important that you learn how to trust the information that you receive and communicate it rather than spend too much time on the techniques.

As your trust in yourself builds, you will begin to develop your own techniques.

Communicating on your own
Single player

The single player game is great for those who would like to make a connection with deceased loved ones on a more private level. If you are reading this book out of curiosity or to connect in a more personal way, you'll find that communicating on your own or as a "single player" will work best for you.

Communicating on your own is just as it sounds. Communicating by yourself and for yourself. It can be challenging to trust that the messages you receive are accurate, when it is just you and the deceased loved one that you are connecting with and it is common to wonder if you are truly communicating with them or instead imagining it based on your memory of them when they were alive. If you can get past that, you'll have the opportunity to connect with your loved ones on such an intimate level, assuring your very soul that they have not left you.

I was very close to my grandmother and was lucky enough to have her in my life until I was well into my twenties. In fact, she lived long enough to know my children and I would take them to visit her on weekends, much like my parents did when I was a child. It was difficult for me when she died because I had stood vigil with her during her last days of cancer and had expected to be the one with her when she crossed, but as luck would have it, the night she passed away was the one night that I was not by her side.

I was finally able to make the one hour trip back to her home in southwest Florida the next day. I visited with my aunt, who had flown in to town the night before and then decided to settle in on the couch that she had took her final breaths on. I fell asleep there.

She communicated with me through spirit that night and if it weren't for the words she spoke - I'd have thought I was only imagining her in my mind.

She spoke to me in Italian, a language that she had tried to teach me when I was younger and that I failed at learning, miserably! She said "clique a-la don" and I responded "clic a ladon?"....she shook her head and said "NO..."clique a-la don" . I know it looks french...but the words were spoken to me Italian. We went back and forth like this, for what seemed to be the entire night and until I was able to pronounce it right. When I finally repeated the words back to her properly, she smiled and left.

It wasn't until years later, when I learned what those words meant....they mean "Gleam of my eye" (or something of the sort) words that Italian grandparents will use to express their love of a grandchild.

That was the only communication that I have had with my grandmother since she has crossed over into the spirit realm, but I feel her energy and love with me always.

More advanced readers may choose to use the method of communicating with the deceased on their own when connecting for someone else that lives at a distance or for an email reading. In general though, it will work best when done for yourself.

The best tools to use when communicating with the deceased on your own include using a pendulum, automatic writing, tarot/playing/oracle cards and psychometry. Some people are able to use the Spirit/Ouija board on their own and if this resonates with you, you are welcome to try this way as well.

To start, sit quietly and bring your focus inward while holding the tool that you will use to receive messages. Ask, either to yourself or out loud, if there is anyone from the spirit realm that would like to communicate with you.

After a few minutes, the tool that you are using will start to move unless you are using cards. For tarot/playing oracle cards, you'll want to shuffle the cards while you turn your focus in and begin your desired layout when the feeling is right.

Just be one with that tool for a while, allowing all that comes to flow through you and into the tool that you are using, allowing your own body to become a channel for the messages. It is also a great idea to record the session if you are able. I have had many experiences where I could actually hear another voice or interesting sounds on the recorder after the session.

Once the line of communication is open you may even begin to see, hear and feel information as well. Just go with it and trust completely.

Conducting a professional reading
Two players

A professional reading is a way for you to communicate with the deceased for an individual person. The idea is for you to make the connection on their behalf and translate the messages from their deceased loved ones to them.

You need not be a professional psychic to do this. In fact, you do not even have to charge money for the service if you'd rather not. I do however, believe in fair exchange of energy and if you decide not to charge money, at least offer a trade or give it to the universe as a gift, knowing it will be repaid to you by the universe in some way.

The best tools to use when conducting a professional reading for an individual include directly channeling the information, the pendulum, tarot/playing/oracle cards, The Spirit/Ouija board, a séance, psychometry and automatic writing.

To start, sit across from the person that you will be reading for and open your connection to them. You can do this by reciting a prayer, using the pendulum, meditating on an item that they have brought you, or by holding their hands in yours.

To communicate with a specific deceased loved one for the person, either ask if they would make their presence known or focus on the energy of an item that belonged to them.

If the person you are reading for does not have a specific person that they would like to connect with, ask if there is anyone present that would like to communicate.

Take your time. When you are first starting out, it can take a few minutes for you to connect with the spirit realm. It can also take a spirit a few minutes to adjust to the method that you are using, align with your energy or it may even be their first time communicating as a spirit.

Trust everything that comes in and try not to ask questions but instead make statements like "I see a red ball", or "I feel like I am far away".

If you are using a tool other than yourself to make contact (for example: A pendulum, Tarot cards or automatic writing.) , ask the questions and accept the answers as they come. If an answer does not seem to make sense to you, do not disregard it. It could be a valuable clue for the person you are reading for.

If the answers do not make sense to the person you are reading for, ask for clarification instead of asking the question again. This gives the deceased an option to present the answer in a different way.

Don't be afraid to ask the person that you are reading for if the information makes sense to them. Oftentimes clarification from the living can open up the channel to their deceased loved one even more and make for a better experience.

Sometimes it is a good idea to simply ask the deceased to give you a message to relay to their living loved one. These messages can be extremely healing and empowering for the individual.

Conducting a gallery style reading
Multiple players

A gallery style reading is when you open up your psychic channel for a group of people, usually communicating with one spirit at a time and delivering their messages to a loved one that is present.

This is a great way to gain experience and to work on perfecting your skills as a channel/medium because you won't be pressured to make a specific connection.

The best tools to use when conducting a gallery style reading is to directly channel the information or conduct a séance.

To start, you'll want to bring your focus inward and ask if there is a spirit that would like to communicate with a loved one that is present.

If you have decided to go for it and directly channel the information, it is best to have the group that you are reading for sit in a circle or in rows in front of you. You can sit or stand depending on whatever is most comfortable for you. When a spirit wishes to communicate through you, you'll begin to see images in your mind's eye or hear/feel something significant.

The deceased will also direct your attention towards the area where the person that they'd like to communicate with is sitting. You could start this dialect by saying something like "I see a young man, in his twenties. He'd like to communicate with someone over here" while you point in the direction that the energy is coming from. You could then add what he is showing you. "He is showing me a small fishing boat". The more you talk about what you are experiencing, the stronger your connection to the deceased will become and before you know it, you'll have honed in on the person that he/she is attempting to communicate with!

Continue in this manner until either the scheduled time for the gallery reading is up or until you no longer feel a connection to the spirit realm.

Conducting a séance is quite similar in that you are not pressured to contact/communicate for one specific person. You'll want to start it out the same way as if you were channeling the information directly, only follow the outline for a séance and have everyone sit in a circle or around a table.

Close your psychic channel

No matter which type of reading you give, it is important to close your psychic connection when you are finished. This is a step that most people will skip and one that I believe is of utmost importance.

If you make the mistake of leaving your psychic channel open after doing a reading, you run the risk of picking up all kinds of energetic junk.

This energy can be caused by residual energy from the reading or can be picked up anywhere else throughout your day to day activities. This energy, at the very least, can leave you feeling tired and drained.

The easiest (and quickest) way to close your psychic channel is to have something to eat. The psychical action of the digestion process, seems to immediately bring a person back to center. Another effective way to close of the psychic channel is to do exactly opposite of what you did to open it. If you said a special prayer, create another one thanking your guides and directing your focus on closing up the psychic channel.

I like to use my pendulum to close my psychic channel when I am finished. I hold my pendulum in my hand so that it hangs just above my lap and instruct my pendulum to close up my psychic channel. My pendulum will move in a counterclockwise manner, coming to a complete stop when the process is complete. It is amazing to watch as it spirals inward from the large spiral that it starts with.

As I mentioned earlier in this book, my psychic connection is always open, but closing off the channel for me will seal it off enough that I am not frazzled. I cannot tell you how many times my husband and I would hurriedly pack up from a psychic fair, hoping to beat traffic and get on the road home after a long day or weekend. In many of those cases, we'd begin to pack up as soon as the last reading for the day was done and by the time I'd even think about closing off my energy, we'd be well on the way home.

My husband will tell you that to have a conversation with me during the times when I "forgot" or didn't have the time to close my psychic channel, was quite a challenge. For me the challenge would be to focus enough so that I could understand what he was saying. Answering something as simple as "What would you like for dinner?" became a task and instead of answering the question, I'd just stare at him with a confused, glazed over look.

I don't do that much anymore. The recovery

takes too long and it is much easier for me to take the extra few minutes to close off my psychic channel when I am finished for the day.

Clear the reading space and your tools

Just as any other game, you'll want to clean up when you are finished playing charades with the deceased. This helps to keep your space and tools in good shape so that you will be able to have a good experience for years to come.

I know many people who create an entire ritual around the clearing of their psychic area as well by walking around the space, clearing the energies and thanking the deceased as well as their spirit guides for their assistance and presence. You can do this as well, if you feel like it resonates with you. I believe that it is all about the power behind the intentions that you set out and if a ritual is going to help make your space clearing more powerful for you, go for it!

When I am finished with my readings for the day, I will simply clear the space by using my Reiki symbols for clearing and smudge the area if it has been a 'busy' psychic day.

The best advice that I can give you is to do it often. Take the time out to communicate with the deceased as often as you are able and your psychic channel will open and expand. The more your mind is accustomed to making a psychic connection, the stronger it will become. As the connection becomes stronger, you'll be better able to know your personal tells, recognize specific spirit energy and become stronger as a psychic.

Chapter 10
ADVANCED DEVELOPMENT

Some of you will realize an amazing transformation in your life as well as your abilities to communicate with the deceased. Your psychic channel will open up and become stronger at the speed of a wildfire. For those of you, I send my congratulations and well wishes with all that you do from here on.

For the rest of us, fully developing the psychic channel may take some time and practice. Even though mine was open at such a young age, it still took me years to fully understand, expand and develop it. In fact, I am still and always will be developing my skills as a psychic.

Whether your channel opens up like a floodgate

or trickles like a babbling brook, I'm sure that you will soon be ready for some tips on advancing your psychic development. I know I wish I had a reference book like this to help guide me through mine!

First and foremost, allow yourself the time to know your spiritual self enough that you fully trust the information that you receive. I know I sound a bit like a broken record here, but trust is the very foundation of psychic mediumship. This is something that I cannot do for you or guide you towards. It is something that will come with time and practice. So be sure to practice often and compare your experiences.

Secondly, let go of your fears. The last thing that a loved one wants to do is to scare you. If they sense that you are frightened, they will pull back their energy and eventually break the connection. Sometimes for good. I had ignored the spirits in my room out of fear. Who knows how the pages in this book would have turned out had I not been afraid of them and shut them out.

Something that happens to me a lot is that I will have people come to me who are dealing with children that are experiencing similar things that I did as a child. They see, hear or feel the deceased among them or at nighttime, when they are trying to sleep. I always encourage them to talk to their children about the spirits as if they are real people and give them some pointers on how they can teach their children to play charades at a young age.

Children who learn how to properly communicate with the deceased at an early age, are able to release their fears early, thus raising their spiritual vibration. My specific advice is to ask the deceased what it is that they want, or why they are coming to you unannounced. Also know that you can tell them that they are frightening you by coming to you in the way that they are, i.e., nighttime, moving items in the home, showing you what they looked like in their final moments.

Yes...of course those things are going to scare the crap out of you. We are programmed at an early age to be afraid of the headless man in horror films and zombies! We are programmed to fear all of the things that we do not understand.

Fearlessness is key to a strong psychic connection. I once knew a woman who was filled with enough fear that someone had put a curse on her that her tongue swelled up inside her mouth so bad that she couldn't read professionally for a week! I often wonder if it was the curse that caused the swelling to get so bad, or her own *fear* of the curse that did it.

Here is a great fear releasing visualization that I wrote especially for you...enjoy!

Sit quietly for a few moments and bring your focus and attention inwards. To do this, you can focus on your breathing, as you breathe in an out. Or you can visualize your body from your mind's eye and from head to toe.

Take in three slow deep breaths and allow yourself to relax a little more with each breath that you take.

Imagine that you are standing in front of your greatest fear of this moment in your life. (you can use this visualization for any fear that you may have, but for this exercise you can imagine a fear that you have around communicating with the deceased.)

Immediately surround yourself in a protective bubble. You can imagine that the bubble is made of anything that you like, so long as you can see through it. I like to imagine plexiglass, but you can imagine clear plastic, an energy bubble or whatever you'd like.

Once you are safe inside the bubble, Imagine what your fear would look like if it were a baby and watch it as it shrinks down to baby size before you.

As you watch the fear shrink down to baby size, you'll begin to realize that it has less power over you. Continue to let it shrink until it is completely gone.

This make take a few times before it happens naturally when you are feeling frightened, but is very effective when you practice it regularly.

Another great way to advance your psychic connection is to meditate on your pineal gland. The pineal gland is a tiny gland that is located almost directly in the center of your brain. This little gem has only been recently recognized scientifically and is the gland that is associated with psychic activity.

It is energetically aligned with the third eye chakra. You can find loads of helpful resources online when it comes to clearing and activating this gland with foods, herbs and mental exercises.

I like to utilize meditation and hypnosis when working with the pineal gland. Most people have experienced amazing results using my psychic activation meditation and workbook.

You can find tips on the best ways towards creating a healthy pineal gland, assuring that your psychic channel is functioning at its best. One of the things that I suggest in the workbook is to cut back on foods and products that are high in fluoride. Too much fluoride in the bodies system can cause a buildup around the pineal. This buildup has been proven to cause a multitude of disorders that include, sleep disorders and creating a block to the area of the brain that controls the psychic channel.

Learning how to reach a light meditative state quickly and effortlessly is going to be a key to making a good strong connection and is also good exercise for your pineal.

Knowing the way you process your life experiences. (see the exercises in chapter two) is going to help you immensely when it comes to learning about meditation. Much of the teachings on meditation today leans towards teaching you how to visualize something in your mind's eye and while that will be helpful for those who process their life experiences by *seeing* them in their mind's eye, it does little to nothing in helping those *who feel, sense or hear* things.

To best strengthen your ability to meditate, allow yourself to experience something small at first. Experience it with all of your senses. You will naturally gravitate to the one that works best for you. The following is a great mediation that not only helps to strengthen your meditative mind but can also help accelerate the pineal gland.

Sit quietly for a moment and focus on the area in your mind, where the Pineal Gland is located. Allow yourself to psychically connect to the gland, noting its current shape, size and vibrational frequency.

Now imagine that it is growing and vibrating at a higher frequency than before. Allow this to occur until it is the perfect shape, size and vibrational frequency for your psychic advancement.

When you are finished, write down your experiences. Do this once a week for as long as you'd like and compare you notes to find any changes that occur as your intuition develops!

THE ANTAHKARANA MEDITATION
Meditating on the Antahkarana symbol can also help to fine tune your pineal gland. In Hindu philosophy, the word Antahkaran refers to the totality of two levels of mind, namely the intellect or higher mind, and the middle levels of mind which, according to theosophy exist as or include

the mental body. Antahkarana has also been called the link between the middle and higher mind.

It is believed that this symbol is multi-dimensional and is also used by healers to help activate healing at a higher plane of awareness.

How to meditate using the Antahkarana symbol:

1.Gaze steadily at the image for 10 – 30 minutes.

2.Gently push away any thoughts that may come up

3.After a while, the image may begin to shift or fade in and out, or it may disappear completely. If this happens, it is a good thing, meaning that you have entered into a deeper level of meditation – so do not allow this to distract you.

4.Daily practice can help you develop your mental clarity and fill you with a sense of peace and oneness that will carry throughout the day.

If you enjoy sharing your experiences and your spiritual journey with others, you can advance your psychic development by joining a group or class. There are plenty of mediumship study groups and classes out there where you can get together with people who are at various stages in their psychic development. In fact, you can find most of them available online where you won't even have to leave the house!

Some great resources for finding a group or class to join include:

bodymindspiritdirectory.org (US)

This is my favorite website for psychic/spiritual resources. Here you can find psychic/spiritual events, classes, brick and mortar storefronts as well as online events and classes...all in your area!

Unfortunately, this site is only US based. If you live in a country other than the U.S., I'm sure you can find a similar site by searching the internet for a spiritual directory in your country.

meetup.com

Meetup is the world's largest network of local groups. More than 9,000 groups get together in local communities each day, each one with the goal of improving themselves or their communities. You can either create your own group or find one of the thousands already meeting up face-to-face.

Keep in mind that most meetup groups meet in person, so be sure to practice safety above all. I would advise meeting up with a group that meets at a public place if it will be your first time meeting with them.

groups.google.com

Joining a google group is a great way to get together with others across the globe and from the convenience of the internet.

You can even access your group from your mobile device if you are away from home. Joining a google group is a great way to test the psychic waters. As with meetup, you can form your own group or join an existing one.

Your local new age/spiritual shop

This is a great option if you would like to attend a workshop or class in person. All you need to do is go to your local new age/spiritual shop (there seems to be one in every nook of the world lately!) and ask them if they offer any type of psychic development/meduimship classes. Chances are, they do and if they do not, most will gladly point you in the right direction.

shop.mindtripproductions.com

I wouldn't be a good hostess if I didn't tell you about my website. Mind Trip Productions Digital Bistro offers an array of digital products from some of the leading spiritual leaders and advisers in the community.

Here you can find audio classes, video classes, e-courses and more. Digital learning has become the new way to learn and is much less expensive than going to a traditional in-person class.

Finally, you could learn self-hypnosis or visit a spiritual/intuitive hypnotist to open your psychic channel more. I have been a certified clinical hypnotist since 2000 and have been witness to some amazing spiritual and psychic shifts as a result of hypnosis.

It is important to note that although similar, hypnosis and meditation are different in the way that we speak to the subconscious mind once a relaxed state is met. With meditation, one simply allows the subconscious/super-conscious to have an experience of its own accord and allow shifts and changes to occur.

With hypnosis however, the subconscious/super-conscious is specifically directed to respond a certain way thus instructing the shifts and changes to occur. There is no wrong or right way and both can be a great tool to use towards accelerating your psychic channel.

The reason hypnosis works so well for psychic development is because you can gain immediate access to the super conscious mind and program it to accelerate your psychic development.

The super-conscious is the part of the brain that can access the higher self/spiritual self and facilitate communication with the deceased. I like to focus on the pineal gland when working with my psychic clients and have created a 28 day hypnosis program called psychic activation. In this program, I cover all sorts of ways to open and enhance you psychic abilities, from foods that feed the pineal to gemstones that help facilitate psychic activity.

Mostly, I focus on how easy it is to open up this channel by using hypnosis.

Hypnosis visualization to help open (or close) the door to the spirit realm

(this visualization can also be used to help close the door for a child or if your psychic channel is opening up faster than you are comfortable with.)

Start by taking three deep breaths – breathing in through the nose and out through the mouth.

On the first breath in and out – allow your body to relax as you listen to the sound of your breath...in and out.

On the second breath in and out – imagine that you are inhaling white relaxing light and exhaling dark negative energy...in and out.

And finally on the third breath in and out – imagine that you are breathing in peace and comfort and that your body relaxes deeper as you exhale...

Using the processing system that works best for you, imagine that you are standing at the top of a large spiral staircase. As you look deep into the stairwell, you know that it will lead you to the place where all of your psychic abilities are kept, including your ability to communicate with the deceased.

Follow the stairs down and as you do, count the stairs backwards. I do not know which number that you will begin with because this is your own unique stairwell and only your subconscious knows how many there are. Simply start with the first number that comes to you...and count backwards.

10...9...8...take a step down with each number you count. When you reach the number one, you should be at the bottom of the stairwell.

Imagine that there are many doors directly in front of you. One for each of your psychic abilities. Some may be closed completely, because you have chosen not to use that gift...some are open a little...while others may be open wide.

Locate the door that contains your psychic ability to communicate with the deceased. Notice if it is opened a little or a lot, or if it is closed completely.

Now walk over to the door and adjust it, so that it is opened (or closed) enough that it allows for the perfect channel of this psychic gift. You will know when it is just right.

Know that you can return here anytime that you would like to adjust the flow of any of your psychic gifts. When you are finished, walk back up the stairwell to bring yourself back to full consciousness.

Practice this visualization as often as you'd like to help open up your psychic channel. In time you may notice that your walk down the stairs is shorter.

Feel free to try all of the techniques here that you think might help you with the further development of opening your psychic channel and communicating with the deceased. When practiced regularly, they will surely help expand your awareness of the spirit realm.

In closing, if you find something here that resonates with you, try it. If it works for you, stick with it and if it doesn't, then disregard it. The most important thing to keep in mind is that this is your journey, not mine and not everything that works for me will work for you. This is one of the many reasons that I love the psychic/spiritual world so much! With practice, you will begin to develop and create your own methods, tools and techniques that will make your game of playing charades with the deceased a unique and empowering experience for you.

ABOUT THE AUTHOR

Michelle Meleo

Michelle Meleo was born and raised in Lakeville, Massachusetts, a small New England town just outside of Plymouth, Ma. Michelle has been aware of her psychic abilities since childhood and has spent most of her life developing those skills.

She believes that everyone has the capability to access and develop psychic skills for personal as well as professional uses.

In 2000, Michelle received her Clinical Hypnotherapy Certification and began creating CD's and mp3's as Mind Trip Productions. To date, Michelle has created and published numerous works that include hypnosis programs, easy to understand workbooks and hypnosis recordings to help others recognize and develop their own psychic skills. She also has created hypnosis products for weight loss, stress relief, finding prosperity, reducing physical pain, sports and athletic enrichment, overcoming addictions, improving skills and performance, spirituality, loss/dealing with grief and sleep enrichment.

To learn more about Michelle, visit her professional website; www.MichelleMeleoOnline.com

More publications by Michelle:
- Your Four Steps to Success 28 day program
- Psychic Activation Hypnosis Program
- The Prosperity Mind Hypnosis Program
- Quick & Easy Weight Loss Program
- Enhance My Calm Hypnosis Program

Accreditation's:
- Certified Clinical Hypnotist(ABH)
- Naturopathic Doctorate 2000 (AINH)
- Chinese Holistic Therapist 2000 (AINH)
- Reiki Master/Teacher/Usui system 2001
- Professional Psychic
- Ordained Minister (ULC)

Michelle's Websites
- MindTripProductions.com
- MichelleMeleoOnline.com
- Shop.MindTripProductions.com
- MasterMinds.MindtripProductions.com

PLAYING CHARADES WITH THE DECEASED

AFTERWORD

As I wrote this book, I shared some of the stories that I was writing about with my family and close friends. I was amazed at the response from those I hold most dear in my life and even more amazed by how this book brought us even closer together than we had been before.

For example, I had no idea that my mother keeps fond memories of visiting her aunt Alice and using the ouija board with her to communicate with a young boy.

Apparently her aunt used the board regularly and kept it out on a table so that it was readily available, whenever she wanted to communicate with the deceased. My mother could not remember the boys name but it was great to hear the stories of her childhood memories of making spirit contact and hearing here perspective about the psychic experiences in our own home when we were growing up.

My mother also remembers the night that I came down stairs to inform her that there were ghosts in our house. She told me that she believed that the house was haunted, but didn't want me to be frightened about it and responded by saying; "You're not dead are you?" and I said no. "And are they hurting you?" I said no again "Then learn to deal with them...and go to sleep!"

The topic of psychic phenomena has now become a regular discussion that starts with someone asking "How's the book coming?" and I have come to realize that having the ability to communicate with the deceased, is a gift that brings everyone together. We forget about all of the silly little *things* in life and begin to really think about the spiritual part of our selves. It's assuring to know that there is something else, no matter your religious beliefs.

I also had the opportunity to learn that many of my clients and friends, share with me similar childhood experiences with spirit communication and It's become a confirmation for me that I have made the right choice in writing this book.

I have heard again and again from those who could relate to spirits whispering or talking in their left ear and from numerous others who have shared their own ouija board disaster stories with me. One of my friends went so far as to tell me.."oh my gosh, you have written my story too!

There were also many occasions in this book, where the deceased would help me along as I wrote about their story and other times when I believe the information that I wrote about was channeled directly through me from a much higher source.

It was truly an amazing experience for me, but there is one specific experience that really stands out in my mind and that I feel is important for me to share it with you. About a year ago my connection to spirit began to become more intense. Spirit energy would come through so strong, that it would make me yawn.

I realized recently that this had been happening because I was beginning to go into a deeper state of awareness during my readings. While writing this book, some of the messages from the deceased would come through during my professional readings as if the spirit of the deceased themselves were channeling their messages directly though me – cutting out the extra time for me to translate what they wanted to say.

It was during one of these sessions, that a mother came through for her daughter to deliver her an important message. I was so amazed by the clarity of the message that I asked her if I could share it with you. With her permission, I have typed out a transcript of the audio recording. I have only changed some of the words so that the message can be universal to all. Otherwise, this is the actual channeled message.

I leave you with this powerful message from (and for) an amazing woman. May it bring you closer to understanding and healing from your own losses.

March 5th, 2014

When we leave our bodies,we're not gone. Our souls live forever, we still have this consciousness. The only difference is that we can't communicate with you anymore by using our hands to touch you, our eyes to see, or vocal chords to speak.

Know that we are always here with you even though we are no longer in the psychical form. Know that we are your family and we will always be familiar to one another. We will always be a part of your soul and we have had many human experiences together, over and over again before this one, and we will do this again sometime soon.. We will be together again.

The bodies that we use are only shells. They're capsules that we temporarily occupy. Through evolution we've been trying to make the human body live longer. When the body is no longer giving our spirit a good quality of life, we simply "pop" out of it and pop into a new one, to once again enjoy human interactions with our soul families. and we shall continue to be reborn and spend more time in the human form together.

Allow your soul to remember why we are here.

Allow yourself to enjoy every moment of this lifetime so that your souls journey may be fulfilled until we meet again.

Made in the USA
Charleston, SC
02 May 2014